CONSUMER INDIA

Inside the Indian Mind and Wallet

CONSUMER INDIA

Inside the Indian Mind and Wallet

Dheeraj Sinha

WILEY

John Wiley & Sons (Asia) Pte. Ltd.

Other Wiley Editorial Offices
John Wiley & Sons, 111 River Street, Hoboken, NJ 07030, USA
John Wiley & Sons, The Atrium, Southern Gate, Chichester, West Sussex, P019 8SQ,
    United Kingdom
John Wiley & Sons (Canada) Ltd., 5353 Dundas Street West, Suite 400, Toronto, Ontario,
    M9B 6HB, Canada
John Wiley & Sons Australia Ltd., 42 McDougall Street, Milton, Queensland 4064,
    Australia
Wiley-VCH, Boschstrasse 12, D-69469 Weinheim, Germany

Library of Congress Cataloging-in-Publication Data
ISBN 978-0-470-82465-8

Typeset in 11/14 Sabon Roman by MPS Limited, a Macmillan Company
Printed in Singapore by Saik Wah Press Pte. Ltd.
10 9 8 7 6 5 4 3 2 1

To my father Shri Birendra Prasad and mother Shrimati Lakshmi
To my wife Valerie

CONTENTS

FOREWORD

It's been more than a decade that I moved out of India to the Southeast Asia and, since then, I have had the opportunity of looking at India from the outside. The biggest change that I see in India today is its energy. The buoyancy in India is palpable on its streets, in its boardrooms and in the eyes of every Indian walking the road. Needless to say, this new India is making news all over the world today. As the equation of the world economy changes in favor of India and China, the World's attention is turning sharply towards these markets. While on one level China and India look attractive for their potential, with a closer look they are not so easy to crack. For many marketers brought up in a Western way of thinking, these are comparatively new markets, and consumers in them think and behave very differently. Marketing in India and China is about unlearning our past and learning for the future.

This doesn't however mean that from within, it's easy to understand India. As Dheeraj points out in this book, India has seen unprecedented change in a short time: about 15 years. For people living through the change it generally appears continuous, unless they step out of their lives and look at it objectively. It is important to do this, as most Indian business houses have built their success through the traditional Indian value system. Today, they face the huge challenge of transforming their culture, products and services based on an understanding of this new, changing India.

That India is different and has its own logic is not a new statement. The biggest advantage of this book is that it goes beyond the "India is different, India is complex" argument. It actually pins down what is so unique about the Indian consumer and the market today. Dheeraj has an innate understanding of India's past through its culture, mythologies, and cinema. In *Consumer India,*

he brings alive the change that India is going through in its mind
and the wallet, and contrasts this with the traditional way of living and thinking. The way Dheeraj has woven stories on changing India makes this book an insightful, but more importantly an
enjoyable read.

This is a revelatory book about the Indian consumer and the
market as it illustrates concepts that have never been explained
before with such sharpness. The concept of access brands—
brands that bring consumers membership to categories dominated
by premium and luxury players—is a unique one for emerging markets. The other big feature of the book is that it makes
several complicated issues look simple. The chapter "Branding
the Bazaar" talks about how there is a viable "New Premium"
segment emerging at the top-end of the market and the "Entry
Level" shaping up at the bottom-end of the Indian market. In
chapter Three, "Generations, One Big Market," one finds that
there are only three big consumer segments in India—the No-
Strings Generation, the Transition Generation and the Partition
Generation. If we overlap these two frameworks, we know
exactly where the hot, new opportunities are emerging in India.
For example, the overlap between the No-Strings Generation and
the New Premium gives us a "premium young" segment. This is
a clear opportunity for brands to tap a young population, which
has the desire and the means to live a good life. There are many
such nuggets in the book, which lead us to new opportunities for
brands, and businesses in India.

As Dheeraj has put it in the chapter "Masala Media," Indians
have progressed more than India has. The fact that the Indian
civil infrastructure and government policies have somewhat
lagged behind the personal progress that Indians have made.
Amid all the positive chatter about India and its progress, this is
the biggest challenge for the India growth story to continue. But,
like everything else in India, this too is an opportunity. Media in
India has risen to this opportunity by mobilizing the mass of consumer momentum for causes relevant to everyday people. There
are opportunities for other businesses in helping India cover this
gap between the progress of its infrastructure and the progress of
its people.

The other gap in India is between India A (the urban and affluent India), the beneficiary of most of this progress, and India B (the rural and high-potential India). Bridging the gap in progress of these two sections of people within India is also a huge opportunity for the marketing and business fraternity, especially since projects like the Nano have proved the feasibility of targeting the "Bottom of the Pyramid" as a business model. In the global arena today, I feel proud to be an Indian but the lopsidedness of India's growth is disturbing. I am convinced that strategies to make the growth more inclusive make sense both for our businesses and our souls.

The idea of "complementality" as Dheeraj describes, is a fascinating understanding of how the relationships between today's urban couples are changing, where it's perhaps not so important to be together but more important to be *there* for each other. Similarly, the understanding that in a country where everyone is feeling young, the real youth is feeling squeezed and is looking for brands that are their partners in crime. The overall shift of the Indian mindset from the *Brahminical* (priestly class) mindset to a *Kshatriya* (warrior class) mindset explains at a larger level why all these changes are taking place. These and many such insights power up this book.

Understanding India is not easy. India has opportunities but only if you know how to find them. And most answers lie at a level deeper below. India needs a guide to walk you through and Dheeraj steers you through consumer India with anecdotes and stories from consumers, Bollywood, category data, marketing cases and the macroeconomics of the country. The book is like 10 different stories on the Indian consumer market told in an easy and engaging style. Above all, it presents the most definitive account of how things are changing in this country written till date. India has produced many fine strategic planning minds. This book, to my mind, puts Dheeraj right on top of the lot.

Sonal Dabral
Managing Partner India
Head of Creative Asia
Bates141

ACKNOWLEDGMENTS

This book is a shared dream with those who have goaded me to write one. That it's a reality today is an acknowledgement of their belief in me.

The possibility of writing a book on the Indian consumer market was first discussed with CJ Hwu of John Wiley & Sons (Asia). CJ patiently guided me through the early stages of the development of this book before she moved on to bigger things at Wiley. Nick Melchior has been mature in his advice and accommodating in his handling thereon. I wish to thank Kristi Hein for her efforts at understanding the Indian nuances while editing and Joel Balbin for ensuring a smooth production of the book, coordinating various people and processes.

It can be said that your first job is like your first love; it changes you forever and can never be forgotten. My first six years of working life was spent at McCann Erickson under Santosh Desai (formerly President McCann, now MD Future Brands). The work that I did at McCann helped develop my worldview on Indian consumer and brands.

As I moved on to explore life on my own, Bates141 offered me the playing field to explore new ideas. Bates141 has been a story of my personal transformation along with that of the agency. My ideas and views on the Indian consumer market have grown and matured because of two factors at Bates141—the challenge of building an agency almost ground up and the freedom to dream and implement brave ideas. I want to thank our mentor Ranjan Kapoor and the Regional Leadership at Bates141, Jeffery Yu, Sonal Dabral, Frederique Covington and David Meredith.

I have been fortunate to work with clients who have engaged me in brand and business conversations right from the conception stage. I need to acknowledge the various conversations with clients at Virgin Mobile, TVS motors, Dabur, Cavin Kare, Max Bupa, Marico, Tata AIG and many others that have helped clarify my thinking on brands and the Indian market.

A very deserving thanks to the entire strategic planning team at Bates141 India, who have been with me in this process of understanding the Indian consumer and have humored me on some insane theories and experiments. For the working relationship that I share with them, thanks are due to Sandeep Pathak (CEO, Bates141) and Manosh Mukherjee (COO, Bates141).

Some of the concepts used in the book started to take shape with the papers that I presented at the ESOMAR Asia Pacific conferences. I am thankful to Esomar for allowing me the opportunities to present at these forums and to use parts of the thinking here.

The young and talented art director, Preeti Varma has with much hard work and flair conceptualized and created the cover design for the book.

Valerie, my wife, who has changed various hats from being the bouncing board, the reviewer and to the motivator. She has patiently lived through my mental absence from the house during my writing weekends. She still made sure that I got my endless cups of *masala* tea while I typed the stories of the Indian consumer on my laptop.

Dhruva, my five-year-old son, who could never understand why I can't finish my work at office, has demonstrated unbelievable patience in allowing me to be on my computer despite being at home. He is secretly hoping that I write something as interesting as the Spiderman series.

INTRODUCTION

Dilwale Dulhania Le Jayenge ("The Big Hearted Will Take the Bride"), directed by Aditya Chopra and released in 1995, became the biggest Bollywood hit of the year and a defining film of the decade. In an emotionally charged moment in the movie, Raj (played by Shahrukh Khan) refuses to elope with his heroine, Simran, because he wants her family to endorse their marriage, even though Simran's mother is encouraging him to run away.

Thirteen years later, in 2008, Chopra's *Rab Ne Bana Di Jodi* ("A Match Made by God") became the fourth-highest-grossing Bollywood film of all time. This time around, in a similar movie moment, Raj (played by Shahrukh Khan) asks his heroine Taani to run away with him if she thinks she is not happy in her marriage; he exhorts her to snatch her personal happiness from her destiny. From refusing to elope with his girlfriend to asking someone else's wife to run away in search of personal happiness, the depiction of relationships and morality in mainstream Bollywood cinema has come a long way—obviously mirroring the tremendous change that India has seen in the last 15 years. This transformation of India, which started with its economy, is affecting its sociocultural fabric and people's everyday behavior and consumption patterns.

In *Consumer India*, I take a close look at the new India that is emerging from these transformative changes, tracing our changing mindset and the impact on our consumption behavior. Having established where we have come from and what we are going through, I explore the seemingly complex behavior of the changing Indian consumer, with the goal of bringing consumer and marketer together in one frame.

I

Mapping changes in people's mindsets and behavior is a tricky job. More often than not, we who make the attempt are at one extreme or the other. At one extreme, we live in denial, insisting that the change we see is not widespread—as it happens, for instance, when we talk about rural and small-town India. The changing aspirations of small-town India often surprise marketers who assume that these people are still conservative in their desires. At the other extreme, we end up manufacturing change based on what we see in a small cross section of the population. Cover stories in news magazines that portray typical Indian youth with tattoos, spiky hair, and multiple piercings, and juggling as many gadgets in two hands, belong in this category.

When it comes to understanding change, it's critical to identify its exact nature and degree before drawing conclusions. Cultural and mindset shifts cannot be simply drawn from consumers in focus group discussions or in-depth interviews. The method used in *Consumer India* can best be described as triangulation. The book uses elements of popular culture, observed unconscious behavior, consumption data, findings from our many consumer interactions, and other macro influences to arrive at an understanding of what's going on inside the Indian mind and wallet. Its narrative weaves through examples of Bollywood, our cultural conditioning, today's role models, our behavior as consumers, and the role of brands and brand marketing amid all this.

The consumer interactions referenced throughout the book took place over several years, across geographies and age groups, while probing a particular consumer segment or category. We believe that we must first see consumers as people, not merely as consumers of our particular brands and products. Thus, unlike the typical focus group, these were meant to be conversations with people about larger life themes, in their own settings. For instance, to understand men, we met with their girlfriends and wives to hear what they thought of the men in their lives; we met with youth in their own circles of friends to understand their natural behavior; and we invited mother-daughter pairs to talk together their own lives and what they observed in each other, to understand the changes between generations.

I begin the book by mapping the changing mindset of the one billion Indian minds. This larger cultural transformation is the foundation of how India today is thinking and behaving. Next, I explore the changing meaning system of five key categories in India: money, beauty, media, technology, and retail. I then discuss three critical target segments: youth, women, and rural India. I chose these five categories and three consumer segments for two reasons: first, these are categories of high growth and consumer segments of high significance in the Indian consumer market, and second, their transformation is representative of larger changes in Indians' thinking and consumption behavior. For instance, understanding the changing meaning of money or the way today's Indian youth think has implications beyond the immediate categories of financial brands and youth marketing, respectively. The final chapter offers a new segmentation of India, viewing the complex India opportunity through a simpler lens of three generations.

The book does not generate a checklist of dos and don'ts or a list of opportunities; rather, I have set out to articulate the principles that govern the behavior of Indian consumers. Drawing a list of opportunities should then be an easy mental exercise for the reader. *Consumer India* doesn't hand you the treasure directly, but guides you with surefire clues.

The story of India's *Karmic* transformation told here is also a personal one. Most authors, film directors, and artists have their peak time, when they connect most surely with the rhythms of the time, the life around them. This book is in equal measure an analysis of various cultural and marketing data and a view of India that I have personally lived. As a part of India's transition generation, I have seen us going from Doordarshan to digital TV, from tailored cotton trousers to Levis, from Ambassador to Honda, from five-day cricket matches to T20 cricket, from my parents' attempts at social adjustment to my own desires for shining through, from a childhood in small-town India to a work life in Mumbai, from feeling sorry for myself for being an Indian to being India proud.

This book is a sum total of my experience working on brand strategies for many Indian and multinational brands. How best can we sell health insurance to a country where good health is either a mark of prosperity or blessings from god? How does a culture that has been taught to be wary about money now respond to its abundance—and what implications does this have for finance brands? How do local entrepreneurs react to multi-nationals: do they push back, run away, or simply copy and survive? Does Kakaji Namkeen qualify as a brand? It sells the same wafers (well, almost the same) as Lay's does, gives more value for the money, and spends nothing on advertising. Can a mass brand have a premium offering? What do we expect from technology brands? What is it about caller ringtones that makes them such a success with mainstream India? India is about its large middle-class consumers, but isn't there a profitable premium segment emerging? In a country where everyone is feeling young, what happens to the real youth? Attempts to resolve and understand many of these questions form the staple material of this book. It's a practitioner's account of what the Indian consumer wants—written from the playing field, not the sidelines.

I

TRANSFORMING THE KARMA

HOW CULTURAL FORCES ARE SHAPING
CONSUMPTION BEHAVIOR IN INDIA

A Changing India

There are two reasons for this book. In a world economic environment in which most developed economies are struggling to
maintain a positive GDP growth rate, India boasts an emerging
economy that's looking at an 8.5 percent growth rate in 2010–11.
Although it's critical that the developed markets of the world regain
their health for the rest of the world to feel better, it's also clear
that the current economic crises will certainly shift unprecedented
power and responsibility for growth to the East. India and China
are therefore the two countries expected to power the world GDP
in the next decade. As Indian consumers constitute a market that is
becoming increasingly central to the shape of the world economy,
we need a better understanding of them.

Even before the axes of the world economy started shifting, the
Indian consumer market had been undergoing its own transformation. To be precise, the Indian consumer has been subjected to a
lot of change in the relatively short span of the last decade. The
changes, most of them triggered by the economic liberalization of
the country, have had a cascading effect on the overall affluence
of the middle class and the available choices in business, jobs,
and consumer products. For a nation and a people who have

lived with a comparative lack of opportunities and limited means for many decades, this experience has been nothing less than life-changing. In fact, for the India that had trained itself, socially and mentally, to believe that real fulfillment is almost always nonmaterialistic, opening up of the floodgates of consumerism has been a positive stimulus to its cultural consciousness. In the interplay of consumption and culture, a new value system is emerging in India. An understanding of how today's consumer India behaves must begin with an understanding of the changing mindset of the Indian consumer.

The economic liberalization of India, which began in the early 1990s, has had a profound impact on how Indians live and think. The opening up of the economy has opened up the minds of the people. The emerging Indian mindset has its roots in the *Kshatriya* values of the traditional warrior class rather than the *Brahminical* values of the priestly knowledge class that have previously been the biggest influence on the Indian mindset. The new India has found a connection with its cultural roots in the *Kshatriya* way of life— which emphasizes extrinsic values of action, success, winning, glory, and heroism—in contrast with the *Brahminical* values of knowledge, adjustment, simplicity, and restraint that had always dominated the Indian way of life.

Brahminism, derived from *Brahmin*, is the foundation of the long-established social norms of India. Of the four main castes in the Indian society, *Brahmins* are at the top. Custodians of the religious sacrament, they are deemed to be the learned class of the society who possess the knowledge of the religious text. They are the epitome of simple living, having (ideally) renounced all cravings for the material pleasures of life. The archetypal *Brahmin* wears a white *dhoti* (the Hindu loincloth), reads scriptures, and practices ideals of self-control.

Built around these principles, Indian society over a period of centuries learned to value things cerebral over things material, giving greater importance to the intrinsic qualities of patience, adjustment, and inner contentment. Individuals sought to be a part of the larger whole and abstained from things that could break the fragile social equations. Ideals such as slow and steady, living within means, and correctness over opportunity dominated, by virtue of overwhelming social approval. Excesses of any kind—whether success, material well-being, or heroism—were seen as threats to the society's equilibrium.

Kshatriyas are the warrior class. They represent action, valor, and competitive spirit. *Kshatriyas* were actually the men of action as against the *Brahmin* who were the men of knowledge. Until recently, *Kshatriyas* values have always been overshadowed by the dominant *Brahmin* value system. However, in the changing Indian context, as a formerly more passive and restrained India is opening up to the new influences, *Kshatriyas* values seem to be taking center stage.

This change in the Indian mindset is becoming the cultural engine of the Indian economic charge. Individual energies of the young people are adding up to a greater momentum for the country as the whole. Considering that more than 500 million Indians are under age 21 and the median age of 25 is even lower than in China (where it is 33), the young are quite a force in Indian society. Their changing mindset is redefining what is culturally desirable. The new behavior codes are different in principle from the codes that have traditionally governed. The change is visible in people's everyday behavior, their dreams and aspirations, their career choices, and their overall approach to life. This change appears to be driven by a new core value that pretty much defines the way the new India is thinking.

Karmic Transformation: The New Diving Force

Karma, in Hinduism, is fate. According to Hinduism, our individual *karma* is a function of our fate, shaped by our actions. Traditionally Indians have taken refuge in the idea of *karma*: if one's life is governed by one's fate, not much can be done to change what's writ. But the new India is seeking to transform its *karma*. Today's Indian mindset is a new but true interpretation of *karma*. The emerging belief is that if *karma* is shaped by your actions, then it's possible to transform your being—to achieve the life that you desire rather than humbly live the one that's destined. The India of today is seeking a *karma* transformation. Nothing is writ for today's India. A refusal to accept their current state of being and a burning desire to transform their lives—and a belief that they can do so—mark the spirit of today's India.

The driving idea of *karmic* transformation is manifesting itself in the following five key cultural codes, principles that govern the cultural response and behavior of today's India:

- Activating your destiny
- The new currency of extrinsic values
- The criticality of the last lap
- Finding extraordinariness
- Making use of tradition

These new cultural codes undergird how the nation and its people are thinking today, and they have implications for the products, brand imageries, and stories they are buying into.

Activating Your Destiny

One of the biggest changes in today's India, especially for the younger Indians, is a belief that individuals can break free of their birth barriers. India's newest generation does not recognize any limitations of class, country, or gender in the pursuit to realize its true potential.

This is a marked departure from how Indians have always lived: with an unquestioned belief in the idea of destiny. The omnipotence of destiny tied an Indian to his or her birth variables forever. Profession, marriage, and social circle—were all determined by where and to whom the person was born. These birth variables continued to wield their power over an Indian's life well into the modern era in India, as a severe lack of resources ensured that the average middle-class person could almost never escape the socio-economic bracket of his or her birth. This is no longer so. Indians today believe that they can achieve their desired destiny by sheer dint of their efforts and ability.

This new cultural code is making itself visible in many ways. For instance, the average age of new homebuyers in India is now in the early thirties, and it is declining every year. The India of yesteryear could almost be divided into two halves: those who owned their own abode and those who for almost all their lives could only dream of doing so. If they were lucky, they could accumulate just about enough money by the time they retired to own a modest house.

This has changed dramatically. An Associated Chambers of Commerce and Industry of India (ASSOCHAM) analysis in 2007 showed that the age range for property registration for personal use had plummeted—from the 50 to 58 that it was 20 years ago to a range of 30 to 38 years from the year 2000 onward. Owning your own house at the age of 30 is thus one of the biggest goals that today's young Indians strive for, in their effort to activate their own destiny.

The impact of change is not confined to the upper strata of society. The city of Bangalore in the southern state of Karnataka, for one, has faced a genuine scarcity of chauffeurs. As India's southern populations, in general, are more fluent in English than those in the northern states, most of the chauffeurs working in a city like Bangalore had some fluency in English. The boom in the services sector has meant that anyone who can speak a bit of English and is open to working hard to get trained is much sought after by the business process outsourcing (BPO) industry. Many chauffeurs in Bangalore joined the BPO industry as customer service agents, at salaries four to five times higher than what they likely earned simply driving someone else's car.

The change is visible too in the sheer number of young women joining the workforce and building careers that until recently they could only dream of. One of the most potent symbols of this change is the Frankfinn Institute of Airhostess Training, which has over 100 centers in 95 Indian cities. The institute, as the name suggests, is making it possible for young girls from all over India to take a shot at a career of glamour and independence. The Frankfinn Institute is representative of the flight that young Indians today are taking toward a life that fulfills their dreams and desires, irrespective of their gender, class, and place of birth.

In a *New York Times* story in February 2007, Somini Sengupta writes,

Until recently, many Indian families would have frowned on the idea of a young woman dressing in a short skirt and serving strangers on a plane. But a rapidly expanding economy has helped to transform the ambitions, habits, and incomes of India's middle class in ways that would have been unimaginable just a generation ago, not least for young women. One consequence of India's new prosperity is the hunger among the young to pursue careers that were simply unavailable to their parents for wages that would have been beyond their elders' compensation.[1]

The world has recognized the entrepreneurial successes of people like Narayana Murthy, who has built a world-class IT organization, Infosys, with zero start-up capital but ample ability and confidence. There are many other such stories in today's India that may or may not have made global headlines but embody this newfound ability of its people to knock on the doors of opportunity rather than wait for it to come knocking. One such story is that of E. Sarathbabu, CEO of Foodking Catering Services, which has reached annual sales of $1.5 million. It's just a little ironic that Sarathbabu, whose company now runs food outlets in more than four Indian states (including Tamilnadu, Goa, Andhra Pradesh, and Rajasthan), grew up in extreme poverty selling *idlis* (savory rice pancakes) door to door. Sarathbabu still managed to get into India's premier business school—the Indian Institute of Management Ahmedabad—and later started his own food venture. In a country where national politics is still avoided by the well educated and the intellectual class, Sarathbabu entered politics in the 2009 general elections, with an election manifesto that signed off "vote for youth, vote for good governance."

Indian Idol (the Indian version of *American Idol*) has run four successful seasons as of this writing. In India, *Indian Idol* has been more than just a TV program; it's been a social phenomenon. *Indian Idol* has offered the potential of fame, glory, and success to average middle-class Indians who have the talent but no resources. The first Indian Idol, Abhijeet Sawant, came from a lower-middle-class area in Mumbai; he was born to a clerk in the Mumbai municipal corporation. Abhijeet Sawant is now the role model of all the Indians who believe that one day they will be able to find their calling through the sheer force of their talent. Ability and intellect in today's India are seen as the weapons to achieve a life of your dreams.

The successes on the world stage of Indians in various walks of life is serving as an inspiration for the entire country, bolstering a belief that anything is possible. *Slumdog Millionnaire* did it by sweeping the Oscars; Abhinav Bindra, a 25-year-old shooter from Chandigarh, did it by winning India its first ever individual Olympic gold medal in 108 years in the 10-meter air rifle event at Beijing in 2008. In the same year, 33-year-old novelist Aravind Adiga bagged the Man Booker Prize for Fiction for his debut novel *The White Tiger*. Vishwanathan Anand won the World Chess Championship title in 2007 and retained it in 2008 by defeating Russia's Vladimir Kramnik in a match-play series in Bonn, Germany. Indians today have witnessed all these feats that they once believed were impossible, right before their eyes. If seeing is believing, there is now desire among Indians at all levels of society to go out and make things happen and not sit content with what happens to them on its own. The feeling on the streets is one of genuine optimism, a feeling that it's India's time for a metamorphosis into a world-class butterfly.

The New Currency of Extrinsic Values

The traditional way of living, through the Brahminical values, meant upholding the principles of simplicity, giving precedence to means over ends, and choosing correctness over opportunity. "Simple living, high thinking" and "mind over matter" have been the tenets of the traditional Indian way of life. Content claimed cultural superiority over form. Depth was always better than surface. Classical got more respect than popular. Academics scored higher than talent.

For the first time, however, several years ago, 60 million Indian households (those with cable and satellite connections) were introduced to the term "X Factor" for that indefinable *something* that makes someone a star. The X Factor—or more specifically, the lack of it—was used by the judges of *Indian Idol* to decimate the chances of many talented singers, some with over 12 years of training in classical music. For the first time, the Indian middle class realized the importance of looking good, dancing well, and being stage-savvy. They realized that 12 years of training in classical singing may not be enough to win a talent competition, but being able to perform like a rock star might be. For a *Brahminical India*—which had valued talent over flair, substance over style, and academics over personality—realizing the importance of the X Factor marked a fundamental shift in mindset. The concept of X Factor in many ways epitomizes the second new code—*the currency of extrinsic values*—that is fast taking hold in India.

The changing value system is evident in the ranking of educational institutes, for instance. Jawaharlal Nehru University (JNU) has traditionally been the revered seat of academics in India. The university offers postgraduate programs in social sciences and specializes in social studies. JNU has been the beacon of academic pursuit and has provided the talent pool for the most elite Indian civil services. The crown of the most prestigious institute in India, however, has quietly slipped away from JNU to the Indian Institute of Management (IIM). This is not surprising, because IIM is the institute that has made the Indian middle class believe that they too can have access to an annual salary of $200,000 and a job based in New York or Singapore—if they can crack its rather difficult entrance examination.

Education has now become more a practical than a philosophical matter in India. People have come to value enrolling in a three-year diploma course in IT from a private education player such as NIIT (the largest private player in computer education in India) over pursuing an undergraduate course in economics or biochemistry. It's the salary potential of the course that is determining the importance of an institute, not the depth of education to be gained. This, when formerly earning a Ph.D. or an M.A. was a matter of such pride in India that the initials were placed prominently on the nameplate hung outside people's houses.

The traditional Indian mindset attached little value to things ornamental. On a train journey through the countryside, you would see huge houses, built on large plots of land, neither plastered nor painted. It was important to own a large house; it was not so important to make it look good. Contrast that with the fact that the biggest hooks now used by real estate advertising today are landscaped gardens, Italian marble on the floors, and weather-proofing on the exteriors. The boom in the exterior paints industry in India is certainly proof of a shift in mindset, from an absolute emphasis on intrinsic values to recognizing the merit of extrinsic values. According to a report by the Freedonia Group, a U.S.-based market research firm, exterior paints have been the fastest-growing architectural paint market segment in India, registering around 20-percent annual growth from 2004 to 2006.[2]

Beauty as a category in India has seen an unprecedented boom in the last decade. Although this is in part a function of rising affluence and exposure, a large part of it has to do with the increasing importance accorded to looking good. In one of our interactions with consumers, young men confessed to going through elaborate facial and beauty treatments before an important interview. Not only did they believe that looking good was important for them to feel confident within, but some of them strongly believed that if they looked good, prospective employers would feel they would be good at their job as well.

The India of today places an unprecedented emphasis on extrinsic values. Ends are today as important as means, if not more so. Talent is not considered much of an asset if it doesn't have money value. Success is not just internal; it needs to be celebrated. Life is no longer an exercise in internal well-being; prosperity and happiness must be highly visible. The yoga that helps you attain internal balance must also give you glowing skin. The *Kshatriya* values of winning, glory, and heroism are gradually crowding out the Brahminical values of mind over matter, means over ends, and correctness over play.

The Criticality of the Last Lap

It has been a common refrain in India for many years that the Indian cricket team lacks the killer instinct. We have always produced excellent batsmen, but go-getter fast bowling always eluded us. Fielding in a cricket match has been something that the Indian team always looked at as a low-end, blue-collar job. The best of the Indian batsmen would retire hurt when it came to fielding, to avoid wasting their energy on something so trivial.

Much of this has changed for the current Indian team. The Indian team today is chasing big targets and winning matches that are tight to the last ball. They are going after the difficult catches and trying hard to stop the batsmen from taking even single runs through some athletic fielding. Those familiar with the evolution of the Indian cricket team will know that Mohammad Kaif has repeatedly earned his place in the Indian team with his remarkable fielding abilities. There is no better demonstration of this changing attitude than India's thrilling five-run victory over archrival Pakistan in the finals of the inaugural Twenty20 cricket World Cup in 2007. Clearly a new sensibility is emerging, one that recognizes the *criticality of the last lap*. The change in the team outlook reflects the larger transformation of outlook that India is undergoing. We are realizing, as a community, the value of hanging in there and seeing things through to the end.

The result: although India has always done well in matters cerebral, such as chess championships and mathematics Olympiads, we are now beginning to win medals in intense sports such as tennis and athletics. The role models of this new Indian sensibility are sports stars like Sania Mirza, who picked up the Grand Slam tennis title in the 2009 Australian Open in partnership with Mahesh Bhupathi, and the ace shooter Rajyavardhan Rathore, who won India silver in double trap shooting at the Athens Olympic Games in 2004. Athletes like them have won India accolades in sports in which we formerly almost feared competing.

"Play the game in the spirit of the game," said Jawaharlal Nehru in 1951 while inaugurating the first Asian Games in New Delhi. "Sometimes winning is everything" is how *Chak De! India* ("Go for It, India!"), the fourth top-grossing Bollywood movie of 2007, lured moviegoers to theaters. The movie, which celebrated a radical "come back and win it" attitude, was the story of a coach and his team, ridden with vulnerabilities, who ultimately found their stage in nothing less than a world championship. In *Chak De! India* the Indian National Women's Hockey team fell, got up, fell again, but rallied to victory, decimating some of the most vaunted teams in the world. Audiences were riveted, their hearts in their throats, vicariously seeing themselves make their own personal dreams come true.

The new code, though most evident in fields such as sports, is becoming the dominant approach to life in India. In the few years just before the economic recession in 2007–2008, the entire world witnessed dramatic takeovers by Indian and Indian-run companies such as the Tata Group and Mittal Steel (now part of ArcelorMittal). The sheer perseverance with which Lakshmi Niwas Mittal approached the Arcelor deal—making offers and aggressive counteroffers, parlaying with the involved governments and stakeholders—was a spectacular lesson in the art of last-mile closure. Similarly, Tata, who were hitherto known more for their trust, stability, and size, displayed a bold, new aggression in paying $2.3 billion for the British brands Jaguar and Land Rover. In March 2010, Bharti Airtel signed a deal with Kuwait-based Zain Telecom to buy its African business for $10.7 billion in what's said to be the largest ever telecom takeover by an Indian firm. The spirit of stability has been infused with the blood of aggression, visible in the behavior of these Indian corporations. Indians today are playing to win, casting off the traditional Nehruvian philosophy of "participation is more important than winning."

Dreams in India have never been in scant supply. What's new is our desire and willingness to go that extra mile in our chase and not settle for anything less than gold. Indians today are seeking a way to turn their dreams into reality. This requires brands and businesses not to tell customers to "dream big," but rather to tell them "Here's how we will help you make it happen." India today is resonating with Bindiya's vow in *Chak De! India*: "We may die, but we will not lose."

Finding Extraordinariness

Indians traditionally have placed a huge value on being a part of the collective. Fitting in was preferred to standing out. No wonder white dominated our choice of colors, whether in shirts, cars, or houses. That ultimate symbol of authority and power, the Ambassador car—duly adopted by the government of India as its official steed—was of course white. The first and perhaps the only color we could think of painting our houses was white. If you look carefully, you'll notice that most of the clothes hanging around the famous *dhobi ghat* (the central washing area) in Mumbai are white. White as a color ensures uniformity, allows us to blend in, and express our desire to be understated. In buses and trains where seating space was almost always in scarce supply, saying "we will adjust" was being social and human. An "adjusting nature" (that is, a compliant one) was one of the most sought-after qualities from prospective brides in matrimonial ads. Being part of the whole and not wanting to stand out was almost a socially rewarded virtue.

In a complete reversal, for today's Indian youth the biggest fear is that they will be ordinary. Being one among the many is certainly not what motivates the Indian of today. Fitting in is desirable no more—standing out is. The particular desire of today's youth is to be extraordinary in everything they do. Their dreams are non-linear and are being supported by high starting salaries, easy availability of finance, and an ever-expanding array of consumption choices. In one of our consumer interactions, a middle-class youth proclaimed that his dream was to own four apartments in all the four major metropolitan cities in India. On being quizzed further as to how exactly he planned to achieve this, he had no clear plans, but his confidence and optimism remained unfazed. The path to the dream may not be charted precisely, but the end point of being extraordinary is very clear.

Hindi films are a good barometer of the Indian culture and its mood. One such Bollywood blockbuster is *Bunty Aur Babli* ("Bunty and Babli"); released in 2005, it has been a success across India. At the heart of the story is the desire of a young boy and a young girl to escape Fursatganj, a representative small-minded town, and make it big in the city of big dreams—Mumbai. The most defining moment of the movie occurs when the film's pro-tagonist refuses to go for a government clerk job interview that his father has set up through a reference. His retort to his father is that the job that he has set up for him offers neither recognition, nor fun, nor fame—the three critical parameters that the Indian youth uses to evaluate anything, including a potential career. This set of values is a far cry from the values of hard work, respect, and honesty that the father has lived by, spending more than two decades in the government job of ticket collector for the Indian Railways.

It's said that desire creates its own path; in this case, however, the availability of various platforms and avenues for finding glory is actually fueling the desire. Prime-time slots across channels on Indian television today are filled by reality shows. From singing to dancing to motor biking to romance to cheerleading, every art, for what it's worth, has been converted to a reality show. From *Star Voice of India* to *Knights and Angels* to *Dance India Dance*, reality television has become the platform for average middle-class Indians who would otherwise never ever have been in the spotlight. Television in India is churning out micro celebrities every season and thereby kindling the desire in a whole new generation to give stardom at least one shot, if not more.

Events such as the Indian Premier League (IPL) have also added to the array of opportunities. Suddenly the chances for a cricketer are multiplied by eight, as there are eight state teams playing in the tournament, compared to the former single national team. A growing choice of alternate sports beyond cricket and careers beyond the standard ones like engineering and medicine are increasing the odds of the ordinary middle-class person's becoming a superstar. As a result, the list of most coveted careers is changing too. Media, airlines, hotels and hospitality, modeling, and sports—career options hitherto the choice of a brave few—are finding popular acceptance.

Entrepreneurism in India was traditionally the domain of certain communities and castes. Those involved in businesses passed on the empires to the next generation; service-class parents desperately hoped that their children would get government jobs. However, recently the number of young MBA students starting out on their own is increasing by the year. Some schools, such as the IIM, are encouraging this through the deferred placement options, which allow these entrepreneurs the option of sitting for placements the subsequent year, in case they realize that their venture is not succeeding. The trend is increasing; even established professionals with fairly well-charted career paths are opting out of everyday nine-to-five jobs to chase their own dreams of entrepreneurship, fame, and glory.

The formerly play-it-safe Indians who once strove to blend in and be a part of the social whole are today seeking opportunities that will make them stand out: bring them extraordinariness! We are making our everyday choices in life and consumption based on whether they can help us shine and find stardom. Indians today are seeking their place in the sun, even if only for Andy Warhol's predicted 15 minutes.

Making Use of Tradition

While so much is changing in India, some things are not. Contrary to the oft-expressed fear of Westernization, the younger generation has not thrown away its traditions. They are in fact using tradition to their advantage. India today is embracing the new along with the old, at times using the power of tradition to conquer the challenges of modernity. Tradition itself has risen to the occasion; it is offered as both a weapon of success and an antidote to the stresses of modern living.

A case in point is the expanding market for Ayurveda. According to a report by the Associated Chambers of Commerce and Industry of India (ASSOCHAM) in March 2008, the market for Ayurvedic therapy and products is estimated at around $650 million and expected to reach $1 billion by 2010.[3] Indians today are taking to Ayurveda in a multitude of areas, ranging from health foods to milk food supplements to skin creams to soaps. Retail shops today are laden with Ayurvedic products for everything from diabetes control to skin whitening to dandruff relief. Ayurveda has risen as an antidote to the modern life of stress, its time-tested recipes being repackaged by various brands in modern formats.

Another interesting example of using tradition to advantage is the resurgence of Vedic mathematics. The Common Admission Test (CAT) is the Graduate Management Admission Test (GMAT) equivalent for entry into the Indian Institute of Management (IIM). Unlike the GMAT, however, CAT has an exceptionally high difficulty level in quantitative ability. Vedic mathematics has come to the rescue of Indian students with its shortcut methods to solve complex mathematical problems. The methodology is now being formally taught in many training institutes, which help students prepare for these entrance tests.

Then there's numerology. There is something of a trend in India these days to alter one's name to make it numerology-friendly. Fairly well-educated and modern Indians will suddenly add an additional letter to their long-standing name so that the total number of letters falls in line with the right astrological calculations. Successful filmmakers such as Karan Johar and Rakesh Roshan, and the highly successful television producer Ekta Kapoor are known to have a fixation with the letter "K" based on numerology recommendations. As a result, the titles of all their movies and television soaps start with this letter. This fascination with astrologically enhanced movie titles or individual names is not seen as superstitious or retrograde thinking in this digital age; rather, it is considered a boost from tradition for success in modern times.

In their march to success and glory, young Indians are taking whatever help they can find. Even god and religion are contributing. If it's examination time, it's not surprising to see the queues outside the famous temples getting a bit longer. Newspapers frequently carry stories of highly successful film stars, politicians, and other public figures visiting famous shrines just before an important life event or immediately after a successful one, to get the blessings of the almighty. Today's Indian society is notable for how the role of divine intervention fits seamlessly with the desire to change one's destiny.

Tradition has also come to the rescue of working couples wanting to start a family. The extended family system ensures that the grandparents bring up the children with all the right values while the young parents are busy burning the midnight oil at their offices. The family itself, however, has evolved to give much more freedom to its members. It's not uncommon to see younger people create their own microcosm in a room within the family. Their personal rooms are well stocked with a refrigerator, television, and in some cases, a handy supply of alcohol. The extended family, where it continues to exist, has evolved to give the current generation access to the best of both worlds: freedom to live their own life the way they want to, along with the cushion of a support system. A prime example of honoring tradition when it's to your advantage.

An integral part of the Indian tradition that is being carried forward is the concept of "middle-class-merit"—the hardworking and conscientious spirit of the great Indian middle class that is the source of their success. Cricket champions Sachin Tendulkar and Rahul Dravid, ex-captains of the Indian cricket team, are role models of how sincere hard work and following a conscientious regimen can be a recipe for success. Dravid's media profile is full of stories about how his parents put a big emphasis on their son's getting his studies right and how he never missed school and managed cricket practice along with a "good" scholastic performance. Sachin is famous for his practice sessions with his coach Ramakant Achrekar, who used a one-rupee coin as a lure by putting it at his stumps. The challenge for Sachin was to finish his session without getting out in order to earn the one rupee coin. Legend has it that Sachin earned 13 such coins—and they remain his most prized possessions. There is something heartwarming about the idea of this middle-class-merit and its ability to transform ordinary lives into extraordinary stories.

The belief in its traditions and the power of this middle-class-merit is taking this new India forward. Today's Indians are not discarding what has worked for them in the past. On the contrary, they are enlisting tradition as a springboard into a new tomorrow.

The New Order of Culture and Business

In sum, these are the five new cultural codes Indians are relying on in their pursuit of this new way of life. They are striving to activate their destiny rather than resigning themselves to a preordained fate. A pursuit of extrinsic values has a rightful place in their lives today. They have realized the criticality of pushing to the limits and closing the last lap, of not letting up until they reach the finish line. They are pursuing individual extraordinariness as never before. In this pursuit, they are making tradition an essential part of their success strategy.

Life in India today is an active verb. The new generation is living out the warrior mindset, determined to claim their rightful places by following the *Kshatriya* values.

This has profound implications for people's behavior when it comes to consumption—and thus for the message that brands and businesses need to convey to connect with their customers' motivations. This understanding is essential for multinational businesses and as much, if not more so, for homegrown Indian businesses, because the latter have been built during the post-independence era based on the traditional Indian value system. As these businesses shift gears to enter a new phase of growth, they need to absorb and reflect the emerging new values. As for multinationals, it's important for them to understand ways in which the world of the Indian is changing—and in which it is staying the same. An astute understanding of the nature and degree of this change is critical for brands and businesses that wish to have a direct connection with the lives of these people.

These new cultural codes are already powering several existing and new categories and challenging their marketers to speak to the new mindset. There are categories that were hitherto low priority and are now beginning to report high turnover. Take, for instance, the grooming industry, which is experiencing unprecedented growth in India, with beauty parlors springing up seemingly everywhere. Formerly salon-shy Indians are now experimenting with beauty regimens such as hair streaking.

The market for looking good is not confined to beauty products alone but has spilled over to exterior paints, interior design, and other accoutrements of appearance. The enhanced taste for design and an increased desire for gloss mean good fortunes for better-looking products. Indian players in automobiles—like Bajaj, Tata, and Mahindra & Mahindra, who previously paid more attention to delivering value and functionality based on their traditional understanding of the Indian consumer—are now placing unprecedented emphasis on design. The new design focus of Indian automobile manufacturers is evident in some of their recent launches; for example, the Bajaj Avenger, the Tata Indigo Manza, and the fully redesigned Mahindra Scorpio.

Traditional Indian businesses have realized the need to change not only their product offerings but their corporate outlook and appearance as well. Most big businesses, such as Godrej, Marico, and Reliance, have attempted a corporate brand makeover, trying to infuse their organizations with what we would call some *Kshatriya* values, to add more vibrancy to their look. Such makeovers can also be seen in many large public sector banks, such as the State Bank of India, the Bank of Baroda, and the Union Bank, to name a few.

Other business segments are feeling the impetus of this cultural change as well. A shift in career choices and the emergence of newer fields such as aviation, hospitality, and entertainment has led to a boom in the vocational education market. The market for institutes providing training for would-be airhostesses, newsreaders, and radio jockeys has taken off. So has the market for allied services that support the burgeoning IT industry and other sectors of the economy. An unprecedented number of sourcing and human resources companies have sprung up in India in the past decade. Kelly Services, a U.S.-based company that provides temporary and permanent staffing solutions, has ramped up its operations in India, opening four more offices in the major Indian metros. This is on top of their earlier offices in Bangalore, Mumbai, and Delhi with over 42 Indian companies as clients.

Never before have so many Bollywood movies showcased the theme of transforming one's individual destiny. Movies such as *Chak De! India, Iqbal, Rab Ne Bana Di Jodi* ("A Match Made by God"), *Bunty Aur Babli*, and many others are a reflection of this changing Indian mindset, and their box-office returns are evidence of how the theme resonates with consumers. Alcohol brands such as Signature whisky, car brands like Honda City, and most men's clothing brands are celebrating the newfound success of the young Indian.

The most remarkable change in attitude, however, has been displayed by the Tata Group. The largest business enterprise in the country, Tata has interests in seven diverse business sectors. Tata as a brand, however, derives most of its business from the materials and engineering sector—and thus derives most of its equity from the power of scale, trust, and leadership. But with a feat such as the Nano, a sub-$2,000 car that can comfortably seat a family of four and is compliant with all safety and emission norms, Tata has reinvented the brand. This is the new face of Tata, now known for innovation and ability to quickly respond to new market demands. Nano represents the new dynamic spirit of the brand, which says that Tata will make things happen against all odds. It's the spirit of delivering on the promise of a sub-$2,000 car despite rising costs. And the ability to meet the launch deadline, despite having to shift the entire production facility out of Singrur in West Bengal.

The new Tata is a living example of the larger shift from *Brahminical* to *Kshatriya* values. This is the face of Tata: transforming its traditional image of scale, stability, and trust into a progressive image of action, dynamism, and innovation. In the words of Ratan Tata, the Tata Group chairman and the catalyst of this transformation: "We have two guiding arrows. One points overseas, where we want to expand markets for our existing products. The other points right here, to India, where we want to explore the large mass market that is emerging—not by following but by breaking new ground in product development and seeing how we can do something that hasn't been done before."[4]

It's imperative for brands and businesses seeking success with Indians to understand this larger cultural transformation. As marketers take in how Indians are thinking and behaving today, their challenge is to find out how their brands can play a meaningful role in the lives of the people based on the new cultural codes. The new way of thinking affects not only the marketing of brands and services but also such tasks as attracting and recruiting cutting-edge talent. The younger India today is clearly seeking a much more fertile work environment that offers a nonlinear growth path; a job that brings them not just money but fame and fun as well.

The India story has turned out to be resilient in the global recession, with a reported growth of 7.4 percent for the fiscal year 2009–2010. It's clear that the hardware of Indian economics is finding support in the software of this new culture. It's the power of the larger sociocultural movement that will help sustain the surge and drive India's economic renaissance. This is an India driven not just by hope but also by action, not just by participation but also by success, seeking not merely to live well but to attain heroic stature.

2

THE CURRENCY OF EMOTION

THE MEANING OF MONEY AND THE
MAKING OF FINANCIAL BRANDS

The Carrier of Emotions

The idea of money in India is fascinating because it's driving all the change (well, nearly all) that the country is going through, without in any way undergoing any change itself. In the context of a changing India, where everything from our ambitions to attitudes to attire is under review, the color of money in India isn't changing. The biggest driver of change has managed to keep its own meaning system intact. Money continues to be a carrier of all the traditional symbolisms—if anything, it's on a much bigger scale now.

Money in India is an emotional currency. Every emotion in this country can be enveloped in a transaction. And every transaction needs a coating of emotion. For example, it's a ritual in India to bless the younger ones by giving money. The significance here is the gesture, not the monetary value of what's being given. In the Rs.101 that a grandfather gives to his grandchild, he is delivering more love and blessings than any hundred-rupee note can ever carry. With a Rs.51 gift at the *Rakshabandhan* (the festival celebrating the brother-sister relationship), a brother promises to his sister that he will be there for her come what may. Money in India is not only a carrier of blessings and promises; it carries prayers as well. It is common practice to offer money in denominations that end with one rupee—such as 51, 101, and so on—to gods and at shrines. In these relatively small denominations of money, Indians ask their gods for anything from career success to the well-being of their loved ones to the joys of parenthood.

Money in India continues to be emotional, even in rather naked transactions such as bribing. For instance, when you bribe a clerk to help you move a government file or reward him for an out-of-the way favor, you don't give him money as the incentive for getting the job done—it's customary to give it as the money to buy sweets for his children or the family. In this way, the bribe actually takes on the form of a mutual celebration. Money becomes the vehicle of sharing happiness.

Money in India is still largely a facilitator of relationships, promises, and emotions. In one of our consumer interactions, the most memorable money moments for Indian youth were when they could make a rather expensive *sari* (traditional Indian women's garment) affordable for their mother or when they could buy airline tickets for their parents and book them on a vacation. The first association of money is still one of amplifying traditional emotions and underscoring traditional roles. Jewelry remains one of the top spending categories on credit cards, and a house is generally the first major purchase that a thirty-something Indian makes today.

Played Down in Importance

Traditionally in India, money was seen as a low-end necessity. Intellect and knowledge took cultural precedence over money and material well-being. Saraswati, the goddess of knowledge, was hierarchically superior to Lakshmi, the goddess of money and prosperity. The religious belief was that the two goddesses could never stay together; that is, you could be a keeper of either knowledge or money, not both. *Vaishyas*—the trader caste in the Indian caste system, who were supposed to have a preoccupation with money—were third in the caste order, just above the *Shudras*, the lowest caste. Being a businessman was not a very respectable calling, and large businesses like Birlas supported educational institutions and religious temples, which earned them a more positive social standing.

Affluence in the traditional India remained a distant possibility for the average middle class person. Most Indians were employed in government services or agriculture, where the boundaries of how much money you could make were quite fixed and there could be no major advancement. People's individual incomes generally increased only enough to beat the rate of inflation. Money was abundant in the hands of a very few, while large segments of the society were born and died in the same social class.

The ways of earning money were highly regulated; government salaries had fixed bands that you could never leapfrog, and to start your own venture—like setting up a factory or entering the export import business—you needed government sanctions. This inevitably meant that most methods for acquiring more money were either unethical, illegal, or both. Having an abundance of money thereby implied a negative character. "Money corrupts" came to be the cultural belief, and many Bollywood movies through the 1970s carried the theme of how sudden acquisition of money led to a loss of morality and turned a person's character and life from positive to negative. Most of the Indian cinema through these times also portrayed the admired protagonists as poor in money but rich in values, while the moneyed were portrayed as corrupt, selfish, and heartless. The prospect of going from a scarcity of money to a sudden abundance raised the fear of a loss of self-control.

In a society where a large population segment has very limited means, the conscious social strategy was to shift the focus away from money. Every effort was made to downplay its importance. The common Indian refrain was that money is like dust on your hands; it comes and goes without warning and should not be accorded any greater importance. But putting money in its place was not enough to ensure social equilibrium. It was important to play up the value of things other than money. Thus great importance was given to one's honor, social respect, and the ordinary pleasures in life. "I still do not pick up money that's thrown at me" is a loose English translation of dialog in *Deewar*, a blockbuster movie released in 1975, with Amitabh Bachchan in the lead role. This line became a part of the popular culture and reassured Indians that self-respect, which all of them could command, was more desirable than money, which very few could have.

What also gained currency in lieu of money was the idea of power and authority. So government positions with high power, such as in the Indian Administrative Services (IAS), carried far more value than any counterparts in the private sector. The value of a white Ambassador car with a red light fitted on its roof— which is what these top government officials moved around in—was far higher than that of any other car on the road, even if that other car was more expensive and belonged to a richer owner. With an overall lack of money as a leveler, power became one of the key variables that differentiated one individual from another. Of course, some of these powerful positions were also misused to make more money.

If you grew up in India during the 70s or 80s, chances are that you have fond memories of playing *antakshari* (a family pastime that involved singing Bollywood songs), taking long journeys on the train with cousins and the extended family, munching on homemade savories, or walking in the rain with your loved one sharing a softy (as Indians fondly refer to the ice-cream cone). Most joyful moments in this era happened during times of togetherness and sharing. Getting together with the extended family, including cousins and friends, was always a high point. Most of the successful movies dwelt on this theme, especially the movies from the house of Rajshri Productions, such as *Maine Pyar Kiya* ("I Fell in Love") and *Hum Aapke Hain Kaun* ("Who Am I to You?"), featuring elaborate scenes with popular songs based on family *antakshari* and home cricket. In the absence of money, Indians tried to find value in the intangible celebrations of life.

Similarly, when it came to savings and investments, Indians preferred ways that kept their capital intact rather than those that risked any loss in the pursuit of growth. Except for the trading communities of India (the Gujaratis and the Marwaris), few people really understood the active concept of money—as something that needs to move around in order to grow. The Indian idea of saving meant putting aside sums of money for a designated future use, such as getting the daughter married or buying a house at retirement. Hence bank fixed deposits and government schemes that seemingly provided an assurance of capital preservation were preferred over the stock market, which promised better growth but also carried a risk of loss. Apparently, unpredictability of any kind when it came to money was a scary proposition for middle-class Indians. It was critical that the investment remain solid—thus gold and property remained the preferred modes of investment.

Out of the Closet

The economic liberalization of the country, among many other factors, liberalized the idea of money as well. It shifted the power in favor of ability and intellect rather than birthright or other unfair advantage. For the first time, ordinary Indians saw the possibility of real money as something within their reach. With the influence of global salary norms, sons of average middle-class families could start at a salary higher than their father's salary at retirement. Large businesses such as Infosys and Wipro have been built on knowledge and ability rather than the might of money. Start-ups in IT made entrepreneurs out of young engineers with big dreams but empty pockets, funded by more than willing venture capitalists. The rise of this ability economy changed the face of the Indian employment scene forever and transformed the landscape of many Indian cities, such as Bangalore and Hyderabad, while spawning several new-economy suburbs, such as Gurgaon near Delhi and Navi Mumbai near Mumbai. This was a beginning of a new era in which intellectual prowess, not capital, became a key driver of growth. Money was finally democratized in India, though it had taken more than four decades from the start of India's political democracy in 1947.

Money had come out of the closet, and now it appeared everywhere. General interest magazines such as *India Today* and *Outlook* carried cover stories on how the new generation of young MBAs was being snapped up at exorbitant salaries and how members of the younger generation were becoming shopaholics and living a life based on credit. *Kaun Banega Crorepati* (*KBC*), the Indian version of *Who Wants to Be a Millionaire?*, was the first of its kind on Indian television. A *crore* of rupees (10 million) was a huge sum in India at that time. Up to that point, the average middle-class Indian had heard about winning that kind of money only through the lottery—which, as a game of chance, wasn't really a respectable way to make money. Now, for the first time, you could win a *crore* based on your general knowledge. KBC was the first connection that the larger India saw between ability and unprecedented money, and in many ways between Lakshmi, the goddess of money, and Saraswati, the goddess of knowledge. The connection has now been established over and over again not only by many shows on television but also by the real-life rags-to-riches stories born out of the new economy. The real possibility that talent and ability *can* make you rich and famous is one of the biggest changes that India has seen in this decade.

Another big change in the view of money is its new legitimacy. Money is being openly, matter-of-factly discussed. Whereas 1970s Bollywood movies were replete with the theme that "money corrupts," Bollywood in the 90s made movies such as *Apna Sapna Money Money* ("Our Dream Is Money") that showcase the direct pursuit of money. The difference is apparent in interactions pertaining to money, such as salary negotiations. The current generation in India is quite bold and direct in stating what and how much they want during job interviews, at times much to the discomfort of the elder generation, who perhaps never learned how to discuss money with such candidness. From television to cinema to everyday life, money is now out there in the open in India.

A Life Less Ordinary

In the changing Indian context, money has been one of the biggest change drivers. Its core meaning and the role it plays for Indians hasn't changed much; what has changed in a big way, however, is the way money is being made and its availability. Increasing levels of affluence have made their impact on the Indian way of life. Affluence is helping us live the same lives bigger and better.

The new contribution of money to Indian life today is in making it less ordinary.

Indians have always lived through their emotions, ties, and relationships and have developed a general love for life the way it is. Money has brought the means to better celebrate these things. It has helped rejuvenate relationships by enhancing the quality of time together. Greater affluence hasn't meant living a completely different life; rather, it's about living the same life in a bigger way. Money has been like a soft infusion of joy into the existing fabric of our lives, bringing a certain specialness to everyday pleasures. It has brought music to an otherwise quiet party.

Amplifying the Sounds of Celebration

The new abundance of money in India is amplifying the notes of celebration. We are using affluence to better celebrate our traditions. *Sangeets* (the ritual song-and-dance celebration by the bride's family before Indian marriages) have become more musical, even choreographed, with professional dancers thrown in. *Karva Chauth* (the married woman's fast for the well-being of her husband) has become a full-blown festival, with restaurants like Nathus in Delhi now offering *Karva Chauth* platters for the special fast-breaking meal. Brothers who live far from their sisters can now fly down on *Rakshabandhan* (the festival celebrating the brother-sister relationship), and it's okay to gift your wife with a diamond—as the much-loved advertising of insurance player SBI Life suggests, so what if you have turned 80?

Life with money in India is a romance in chiffon—a la Karan Johar and his movies, replete with all the traditional themes of family and relationships, though rendered with an international gloss. Quite like the *saris* that his heroines wear, traditional yet sensual, fluttering the long nine yards in the winds of Switzerland or Egypt. Incidentally, one of them, *Kabhi Khushi Kabhie Gham* ("Sometimes Happiness, Sometimes Sadness") was positioned as "It's All About Loving Your Parents." But it was shot in international locales like Egypt and London and even the Blenheim Palace in Oxfordshire, England. When the protagonist, played by

Shahrukh Khan, steps out of a helicopter emblazoned with the monogram of his father's company, he runs into the arms of his mother, waiting for him with a traditional welcome. Soon the film cuts to the hero and his heroine sashaying to romantic lyrics in front of the pyramids. Typical of Bollywood, the drama and the emotions of Indian life haven't changed much; they have just been amplified by the Dolby effects of money.

In earlier times, birthdays were a quiet family occasion; birthday parties today are celebrated at nothing less than a McDonald's, and thank-you gifts distributed not only to friends and families but also to maids and chauffeurs. Goaded by clever marketing, Indians today celebrate every possible festival and every possible holiday, right from Christmas to Father's Day. As if our own list of indigenous festivals were not enough, we are now constantly on the lookout for new occasions to celebrate. Be it Valentine's Day or an international soccer match, we'll seize on anything that gives us an excuse for some get-together and revelry—further evidence of how our instinct for celebrations is being fueled by the availability of money.

A Newfound Access

The other interesting effect of this newly mainstream presence of money for Indians is the sheer access to categories of consumer goods and life experiences that they never before had access to. Air Deccan—now a part of Kingfisher Airlines, branded Kingfisher Red—is a prime example of this phenomenon. Air Deccan made flying possible for a large part of the Indian population who believed that never in their lives would they actually be able to board an airplane. The low-cost, no-frills airline brought to the common man a joy that was previously a preserve for only the rich of India. An airline brand with the "common man"—a political cartoon character created by R. K. Laxman—as a mascot became the ultimate symbol of universal access.

The new prevalence of money and economies of scale have come together to make accessible to Indians what hitherto was not. Having a telephone connection was a mark of prestige for a long time. Traditionally, the only people privileged with a landline telephone in their homes were those who held senior govern- ment positions. Cell phones, when they were introduced, carried a similar prestige; the only difference was, these elite held senior positions in multinational corporations. Since 1995, 427.29 mil- lion Indians have become cell phone subscribers. The boom in cell phones has democratized this symbol of prestige. The joy of being connected to their loved ones while on the go is now enjoyed by a larger India, and they are "making the most of now."

The shopping experience of the Indian consumer was until recently at the mercy of *Chotu*, the ubiquitous helper at the neigh- borhood grocer. *Chotu* invariably stood between the Indian con- sumer and her desires. For only *Chotu* had access to what was on the shelves, and the customer had to gain his favor to be able to touch and feel a newly introduced product or the various choices available in a particular category. Now, thanks to the retail rev- olution, middle-class Indians across cities large and small are experiencing the joy of unrestricted shopping, helping themselves to goods from vegetables to clothes, in air-conditioned environ- ments, according to their own whims and needs. The hypermar- ket format has the Indian consumer strolling the aisles with a glee comparable to that of a kid in a toyshop, not bound in any way by the parental leash. The Future Group, which operates over 12 million square feet of retail space in 71 cities and 65 rural loca- tions across India, can be credited, to a great extent, for this accessibility. The group's more than 100 Big Bazaars have helped sweep away the barriers between the consumer and consumption.

Money has made many other joys of life accessible. Take, for instance, the five-star restaurant, which used to be known only as urban folklore. Having been to a five-star hotel and eaten there was, in traditional India, tantamount to having been to see one of the Seven Wonders of the World. The awe of five-star dining has been a subject of many Bollywood movies, which depicted these places as the habitat of the rich and the mighty. The five- star is no longer such a big deal in India. Like many other here- tofore forbidden experiences that ordinary Indians have now laid claim to, five-star dining is today relatively more accessible. Well, at least for the upper-middle-class Indians; they can now be seen celebrating special occasions like anniversaries and birthdays at these places of prestige.

Making the Everyday Special

A large but not so apparent impact of money in the life of India is its ability to make the everyday more special. For those who went about their daily chores in a mundane way, it is as if money has sprinkled a dash of spice into their lives. Average middle-class households now can afford a color television with a satellite cable connection, with 200 channels beamed right into their living rooms. In the past, being able to afford a television set itself was a big deal, and then you had one channel run by the government (Doordarshan) with no more than one 15-minute program per week dedicated to entertainment: a collection of songs from Bollywood called *Chitrahaar* that the entire country waited for all week.

Those were the days when serving glasses of Rasna (a soft drink concentrate) in the evening was the day's high point. Today, average middle-class households are serving up a tall bubbly glass of Pepsi—and not thinking twice before offering you a refill. The glass of everyday affordability and fun has been filled by the newfound affluence. Though it may not look spectacular in comparison to the rest of twenty-first-century culture, when seen in contrast to where the country has come from, it's a big deal. Examples of this everyday specialness are all around us: Pepsi has replaced Rasna, ice cream is gaining favor as a sweet dish, and Indians are embracing ready-to-cook snack foods such as Pasta Treat. Indeed, snack foods are a booming market, with international players such as Frito-Lay and Indian players such as ITC competing for a $650 million ready-to-eat snack market.

Value added services (VAS) have turned out to be a major source of revenue for mobile service operators in India. Dig a little deeper into the phenomenon and you'll find that a major portion of this is from ringtone sales. And significant numbers of these ringtones are being downloaded by consumers in smaller towns. At Rs.6 or less per download, these latest ringtones—which are (what else?) popular Bollywood songs—are a good, inexpensive way to enliven the routine of everyday life. By 2007, mobile music revenue was on a par with the conventional music industry, at around $157 million. These value added services are among the many things working to make an average Indian's everyday life a little more special.

Recalibrating the Ticket Size of Dreams

One of the bigger impacts of the influx of money in India is the recalibration of the size of our dreams and ambitions. A *crore* is no longer such a big amount in India. Television shows give away a *crore* for anything from singing to performing stunts to speaking the truth. Pureit, the water purifier from Hindustan Unilever, ran a one-*crore* safety challenge for proof that no other water purifier meets all the safety criteria that they do. Whether it's the price of a city flat or the salaries in multinational companies, the average size of dreams and ambitions has gone up significantly. Many young executives and entrepreneurs shopping for their first car are choosing a compact (a category also known as B-segment cars), such as the Hyundai Santro and Maruti Suzuki Swift. People are skipping the linear upgrade path and entering categories at a level higher than traditionally expected. Mumbai is typical of other cities; at one point the most popular dwelling was the "1 BHK" (one bedroom, hall, and kitchen); with rising aspirations, now these are considered too confining, and no more are being built. Meanwhile, several real estate developments with multiple bedrooms, some even with an attached swimming pool, are being launched, despite the global economic slowdown.

With money in hand, Indians are experiencing what they always longed for. One common desire has been a foreign vacation—a distant dream for the middle class until recently. However, figures released by the World Travel and Tourism Council (WTTC), revealed that the number of Indians traveling abroad in 2008–09 (April 1 to March 31) reached 10.8 million, which was up by a million over the 2007–08 figure of 9.8 million. According to the report, India is now the third largest outbound travel market in the Asia Pacific region.[1] The dream of seeing the world, which has been far from a real possibility, is coming true for many middle-class Indians.

This change is not confined to the well-heeled. Even those with more modest means have a desire to live well and give their children a future that they themselves couldn't lay claim to. Televisions (with satellite connections), refrigerators, and other such objects of comfort and entertainment are commonplace even in big-city slums. Executives with well-established jobs are relinquishing the comforts of employment to start their own ventures, partly to make something of their own and largely to be able to build the life that they will never attain by working for someone else. Having money is fueling people's desire to live well and find ways of earning more so that they can continuously upgrade their lifestyle.

Signs of this change in lifestyle are visible in macroeconomic numbers as well. Consumer spending on basics has fallen, from 94.5 percent of all spending in 1951–52 to 55 percent in 2008–09, thereby freeing up money for expenditure on other things. Categories like transport, communication, education, recreation, and personal and business services, which accounted for 15 percent of consumer spending in 1981, have risen sharply, to more than 35 percent in 2008. This obviously suggests that money is finally being spent on things other than just the necessities; it's going into education, recreation, and other services. Also, financial assets such as net deposits, shares, debentures, life insurance, and provident and pension funds, which constituted 11 percent of household savings in 1951, now account for more than 43 percent in 2008. The savings rate itself has jumped from 8.6 percent in 1951–52 to 37.8 percent in 2008–09. Not only are Indian consumers spending more for today, but they are also provisioning for tomorrow, at rates that look substantial. (All statistics are based on data presented in the monthly *Macro Track* published by the National Council of Applied Economic Research [NCAER].)

Living with Credit

At the heart of much of this change in India is our changing attitude toward credit. In India, availing oneself of credit and carrying debt traditionally have been taboo, though not without good reason. There were far too many instances of the local money lender pushing unsuspecting farmers into a spiral of loans and interest payments that never seemed to end. *Do Bigha Zamin* ("Two Acres of Land") is an award-winning Bollywood film of 1953 that won the International Prize at the Seventh Cannes Film Festival. One of many films of the time that explored this predicament, it followed a farmer and his struggles to save his two acres of land from being usurped by the local landlord under the pretext of collecting some loans. Culturally, using credit in India has been considered a sure recipe for personal destruction. Debt was a one-way ticket to hell from which there could be no escape.

Times have changed. The home loan market in India has been through a huge boom. In 2006, the housing loan portfolio of banks grew at a rate of 33.4 percent at Rs.53,198 *crores* ($11.5 billion) and stabilized at 15 percent in 2007.[2] Though the growth rate in the subsequent recession has been slower, the big shift is that the concept of home loans has opened the Indian mindset to the idea of credit in general. The way in which credit has taken off in the context of housing is a classic example of how culturally unacceptable ideas become acceptable if they are a means to achieving a larger cultural ideal. Home ownership in India has always been a big dream. In most cases this dream would not be fulfilled until retirement, as it was the retirement savings that was generally used for building the house. But the possibility of owning a house at age 34 (again, the average age of first-time homeowners has come down to 30 to 38 years, according to an Associated Chambers of Commerce and Industry of India [ASSOCHAM] report) has suddenly made the use of credit worthwhile.[3]

Indians are happily taking on Estimated Monthly Installments (EMI) as the new way to carry debt. Just as debt in any form once indicated a path to degradation in traditional India, EMI has today become a symbol of progress. EMI is the device that's enabling a new house, bike, or car, even a new LCD television for most people who may not have ready cash but hope to earn enough every month to pay the loan installments. Credit—in measured doses and for an end that's progressive—has found acceptance, despite the cultural baggage.

Selling Motivation, Not Money

It's apparent that Indians do not understand the idea of money in its transactional form. Money in India is about what it enables. It's always been so. Although so much has changed around the idea of money, this one element hasn't changed at all. Even large cultural taboos around money become seemingly insignificant when money is used as an enabler of a larger cultural ideal or desire. What marketers and advertisers must understand is that in India, it's difficult to sell money directly, bluntly. The money message must convey a loftier ideal—directing the consumer to a larger purpose, a bigger goal, a brighter tomorrow.

Most big successes in the category of finance have been made based on this premise. For instance, life insurance as a category has sold itself not so much as a cover against the risk of loss of life but more as an investment in future potential. As a result, over 70 percent of new premiums come from unit linked policies (ULIPs), which are linked to the stock market, whereas pure risk-based insurance products such as term insurance have a miniscule share of the market. Even on the policies bought, the risk component is kept at a minimum. The life insurance category is commonly sold as a child plan that will ensure enough money for your child's dream education or as a pension plan that will ensure you a happy retirement. The potential of market gains on their investment, rather than a concern for security, is what has attracted the Indian consumer to the insurance plans. The total of life insurance premiums paid has risen four times in six years, from 2002 to 2008, while the number of new policies issued doubled from 25 million to 50 million during the same period, according to the Insurance Regulatory and Development Authority (IRDA).[4]

ICICI Prudential, the largest private insurance player in the Indian market today, is a classic case of marketing insurance in a culturally aligned way. The advertising campaign it ran in the brand's early days likened the act of buying insurance to the marriage vows of the man. The brand used the cultural symbol of vermilion (*sindoor*), which is the carrier of the man's promise to his wife and an integral part of the marriage ritual. Through this symbol the brand promised to be there for her and her protection always. ICICI Prudential sold the idea of insurance through this symbol of commitment. The brand has followed up this stance with several other pieces of communication, the latest a blessing for a long life—*Jeetey Raho* ("May you live long!")—from the wife to the husband.

It is important to understand that Indians like to personalize transactions. Most of the top money brands in the country— such as the State Bank of India Group, ICICI Group, and HDFC Group—have focused on developing a direct emotional bond with their consumers. It's unthinkable in India to have a money relationship with a person you don't know that well. Indians are more comfortable borrowing from and entrusting money to people (brands) we can relate to. The first step to building a money brand and business in India is therefore to start a relationship. This explains, in part, why most of the financial-sector advertising in India comes across as an emotional soap opera.

When AIG launched its corporate brand in India in 2007, it took the stance "We Appreciate the Value of Your Money." The brand celebrated India's relationship with money and the fact that money was actually an emotional currency for this culture. The television advertising for the brand had a take on an Indian ritual: it's customary to give your "first salary" to your parent. The TV spot featured a young kid who gets paid for helping a neighborhood aunty with her shopping bags. He finds his father, who is chairing a meeting in his corporate office, and gives him the one rupee that he got from the aunty. The brand also celebrated the significance of one rupee in the Indian culture, in which adding a one-rupee coin to any amount suddenly gives it ritual power. The print ads made use of the modern version of this practice: readymade gift envelopes embedded with a one-rupee coin. Unfortunately for AIG, as the company was establishing this cultural connection in India and successfully introducing its mutual fund and consumer finance businesses on the coattails of the corporate brand, the international economic meltdown occurred. The lesson, though, is clear: in India, the value of money is much more than the legal tender value printed on a bill.

In India there are many examples of brands going the cultural route when it comes to money. Future Generali, an insurance joint venture between the Future Group of India and Generali of Italy, has leveraged another cultural idea, that of the *shagun*. Broadly speaking, *shagun* is a good omen. The brand in this case celebrates insurance as a good omen to ensure that the happiness of the family lasts forever. Similarly, the global financial services company ING has latched onto the idea that the value of money in India is much more than its numerical value. With a catchy jingle, its advertising underscores the significance of money in India as larger than its cash value.

The discourse around money in India has always been emotionally and culturally colored. In India affluence has been remixed with tradition. Recently, however, there have been some clear changes. First, there is a fresh candidness around the topic; money is no longer such a scary subject. People are more matter-of-fact about money today than ever before. Also, the fear and guilt associated with having large amounts of it have vanished. So have many of the taboos surrounding the idea of loans and quick growth. Money's role in a gradual upgrade of our quality of life and in promising an exciting future has made money more of an everyday matter for everybody. The purpose of money may not have changed, but it has definitely changed the color of India's dreams. The new language for financial brands can come from this new emerging shade of money: more candid, more accessible, and unprecedented in the way it's changing our lives.

3

BEAUTY IN ACTION

THE BUSINESS OF LOOKING GOOD

Skin Deep

In India, beauty has always *truly* been only skin deep. Traditionally, when parents were arranging marriage for their sons, although they did consider the looks of the girl, they gave prime importance to her other abilities, such as singing, dancing, and embroidery. *Gunwanti* (talented) was somehow superior to *roopwanti* (beautiful). The most celebrated goddess in Indian mythology, Durga, is worshipped not for her beauty but for her act of killing the demon who threatened to destroy all creation. Durga is said to have another avatar, the goddess Kali, who is portrayed as dark as death and credited in Indian mythology as the destroyer of the multiplying demon Raktabija. Even in Indian history, the most celebrated woman icon is the queen of Jhansi, known not for her beauty but her valor.

In traditional India, a culture obsessed with things cerebral, beauty has played a limited role. Beauty has never been the foremost social currency, but it certainly was a pursuit in itself for certain class of people. The women of royalty, wives of the rich, even the gods were portrayed as beautiful. Most portraits of Indian gods like Ram and Krishna made them look beautiful in a feminine way, with curly locks, red lips, rounded faces, and their bodies bedecked with gems and jewelry. Thus beauty in Indian society was the domain of the privileged, the realm of royalty, art, and mythology.

Defined by the Face

The traditional definitions of beauty in India were derived from these very ideals. The face was the key index of beauty; the body was conspicuously absent. In fact, it's almost impossible to find a full body portrait of Madhubala, arguably one of the most beautiful actresses of Bollywood in the 1950s and 60s. The quintessential Madhubala portrait is her innocent-looking face with big eyes, a few strands of hair on the face, and a smile that hasn't yet broken. This, in many ways, was also the definition of beauty in traditional India. There were set parameters that made you beautiful—big eyes, long neck, sharp nose, fair skin, long hair, dimpled chin, and rounded body. Either you were born with these and you were beautiful or you had no hope in hell. Classically, the heroines of Bollywood—such as Hema Malini, Vaijayantimala, Meena Kumari, Sharmila Tagore, or Sadhna—typified the beauty made up of these coveted features. It was almost essential that a woman look like one of them in some way to be qualified as beautiful.

Virtually absent in this equation of beauty was any depiction of the body. While the face provided the social identity, the body remained a personal domain. Much depended on the face, little on the body. Heroes with a paunch could, and did, top the Bollywood charts. This was the age of the "chocolaty hero" archetype. Even the heroines were famous more for the dimples in their cheeks (Sharmila Tagore) and fringe-cut hairstyle (Sadhna) than for their figures. The concept of *solah shringar* (the traditionally prescribed 16 adornments for the Indian women) favored the upper torso: only three of the 16 adornments were worn beyond the face and the neck.

In the traditional construct of beauty, body care rituals were conspicuous by their absence. Clothes were used as drapes. The body was hidden. Even the way the *sari* was worn was more like a drapery, with the intention of hiding rather than highlighting. For at some level, the body symbolized pleasure, which needed to be contained, except for legitimate occasions like marriage, when the body got some attention with rituals of *haldi ubtan* (a paste of gram flour and turmeric used to exfoliate) and *mehendi* (henna tattoos). The idea of beauty in the traditional Indian context was thus centered on the face, while the body remained hidden.

From Art to Action

In the 1990s, however, when so many things began opening up in India, the idea of beauty too began to change. In 1994, out of nowhere, India won the Miss Universe and the Miss World contests simultaneously. Middle-class households gathered in front of the TV and watched swimsuit rounds with their families. The prime minister honored the pageant winners as national champions. Suddenly Sushmita Sen and Aishwarya Rai became the role models for mainstream Indian women, who realized the power of beauty in offering women a chance to take the world stage. The idea of beauty was beginning to transform from being an end in itself to being the means to larger ends.

The biggest shift in the view of beauty in India is this transformation from the world of art to the world of action. Although beauty traditionally was a subject of admiration, it was an object of either desire or poetry. It had little or no role to play in the everyday world. Being beautiful was thus an end in itself. In contrast, beauty today is a currency. If you look good, your chances at the job interview go up. You could build a career as an airhostess or try becoming a television anchor. Looking good today is a stepping stone to success.

A mainstream manifestation of this change in the world of marketing and advertising is the brand Fair & Lovely. Fair & Lovely, as the name suggests, promises beauty via fairness—fair skin, that is. In a culture in which arranged marriages were the norm, Fair & Lovely realized that the matrimonial demand for *gori* (fair) girls was high. So for many years the brand addressed the need to make young girls more marriage-worthy. Today, however, Fair & Lovely speaks a completely different language. The brand now gives confidence to young Indian girls to go out and win themselves a place in traditional male bastions. One of its recent ads is about a young girl becoming a cricket commentator spotted by the popular Indian commentator Kris Srikkanth. Fair & Lovely as a brand has changed from using beauty as a trophy to using beauty as a transformational device.

Indians have always valued substance over style, to the extent that one was seen as the antithesis of the other. Now, we see not only that it is possible to leverage our looks for greater success in life, but also that not looking good and lacking in style can actually set us back in the quest for success. It's quite normal today to hear the guy in the next seat at the corner barbershop giving informed directions on facials and bleaching. He could be preparing for a job interview or a marriage—or nothing in particular. There's a growing belief that looking good gives you the confidence to win and affects how others see you. As a 25-year-old said in a consumer interaction, "If you go for a job interview, people see how you look; if you look good, it's easy to believe that you must be able to work well." Similarly, a housewife commented, "When you look good, even the shopkeepers treat you better."

From Two-Dimensional to Three-Dimensional

In a 2006 study of how the portrayal of beauty in popular culture is changing, we looked at the depiction of beauty and grooming in Hindi cinema in the decade of 1960s and contrasted it with the depiction of beauty in today's Hindi cinema.[1]

As discussed earlier, the depiction of beauty in the earlier days was purely facial, hence static. The camera focused on a close-up of the heroine's face, at times with more than half of the song shot from a single vantage point. There was a heavy use of ornaments, and facial expressions did all the work. Most of the songs around the ritual of beauty, such as "*Sajna hai mujhe, sajna ke liye*" ("I have to adorn myself for my husband"), carried a tone of anticipation of the husband, his love, and his approval.

In contrast, the depiction of beauty in today's movies is much more active. The cinematographer uses long shots; facial expressions have given way to body language, seen from many shifting angles. Accessories have replaced ornaments, and instead of anticipation, we get attitude. The depiction of beauty in today's cinema is multifaceted, compared with the single tone of the 60s. Beauty today is set to a beat; in the olden days it was a lyrical melody. The depiction of beauty has clearly moved from being two-dimensional to being three-dimensional.

The figure and physique (of both heroines and heroes), which did not get even a coy mention some years back, are now hotly debated issues when it comes to Bollywood. Not long ago Kareena Kapoor, now a top heroine, achieved the much-coveted size 0 status. For months, the media was ablaze with conversation about her new size. They gave the same treatment to Shahrukh Khan when he developed "six-pack abs" for the movie *Om Shanti Om*, and Aamir Khan when he did the same for his movie *Ghajini*. From primacy of the face to primacy of the body, the measure of what's good-looking is changing in India.

From Held Back to Vibrant

Most Indian women traditionally wore their long hair in braids or a tightly wound bun; only a very few working women cut and styled their hair. But this has become a common practice today. The act of that tight bun unfurling into open flowing hair, is perhaps the biggest symbol of today's Indian woman opening up as a person as well, to her own desires and to the opportunities of the world. Women's hair, when worn loose and free, has connotations of sexuality and desire in Indian mythology and tradition. This style thus indicates a shift from being constrained and held back to being unleashed and vibrantly alive. In a similar metamorphosis, lipstick and nail color shades have moved beyond the classic red, browns, and pinks. So too has the world of hair coloring; from the hair dye whose sole purpose was to keep graying hair black, hair coloring has evolved to adding a dash of zest through various shades and streaks.

Men are taking part in this revolution too; even office-going men have realized that shirts come in colors other than white and blue. Men in pink are no longer an unusual sight in today's corporate India, and women are embracing bling not only in their jewelry but also in their footwear and apparel.

Indians are using new terms for beauty, phrases like "dressing sense," "nice figure," "good personality," "hair color," and "accessories." These were the terms used to describe beauty in our consumer interactions. It's interesting to see how the idea of beauty is shifting, from being all about what you have to being about what you can *do* with what you have. As depicted in the visual collages that women in our consumer interaction groups made, the earlier construct of beauty was about long hair, a flowing *pallu* (the tail end of the *sari*), *bindi* and necklace, being wrapped in the *sari*, and always in the context of the husband. Our participants' collages on the changing idea of beauty, however, represented dusky looks, sinuous bodies, beads and accessories, a certain sense of intimacy and fun, and a play of colors. Clearly, from being held back in earlier days, today's concept of beauty has become more vibrant and active.

Attitude, Accessibility, and Universality

Our conversations with the observers of change in Indian beauty—such as hair stylists, fashion designers, and makeup artists—revealed newer dimensions that are being added to the concept. Attitude, according to all the experts, has become an essential feature of looking good. Designers claimed that they design clothes to suit the attitude of the wearer. Similarly, hair-stylists claimed to recommend a style with the intention of giving the person's attitude a spike. Beauty seems to be taking on a third dimension, which is more about how you carry yourself than what you are endowed with.

The rising role of attitude has meant a rising role for grooming. The way an average person on the road dresses up today is far smarter and more up-to-date than it traditionally has been. Beauty today has become far more universal. Mass production of the props of grooming and beauty is making good looks accessible to the average middle-class person. As a result, there is frantic activity in categories such as deodorant, which has reached a reasonable size of Rs.400 *crores* ($83 million), with many Indian players such as Elder, Paras, and CavinKare jumping in to join established players such as Hindustan Unilever Limited (HUL) and Henkel.

As Clint Fernanades, a stylist who works for Bollywood and advertising, puts it, "Beauty right now is more a mixture of personality with a certain amount of grooming. The basic person who walks on the street has changed from wearing trousers to jeans. Today you don't see ungroomed people and say they are beautiful. Media has a lot to do with it. Earlier it was just kohl and a *bindi*, now it's also mascara, colored hair, and many different shades of lipstick."[2] The impact is visible in the growth of the cosmetics market, which, according to the Associated Chambers of Commerce and Industry of India (ASSOCHAM), will grow from $950 million to $1.4 billion by 2010–2011.[3]

Highlighting Natural Appeal

It's true that India is one of the world's biggest markets for fairness products. Fairness creams as a category generate close to Rs.1,500 *crores* ($310 million) annually, and a significant 13 percent of usage comes from the age group of 12- to 15-year-olds.[4] The lingering cultural desire for fair skin seems almost regressive when compared to the kind of changes taking place in the larger Indian mindset. Although a brand like Fair & Lovely has moved its proposition from the world of matrimony to the world of women being successful in male bastions, the progress is only on a certain axis of beauty. That skin whitening products remain such a huge market in India is evidence of one unchanging aspect of the Indian notion of beauty—the desire for fair skin.

A still-emerging but already definitive new notion of beauty is taking root in India: it is about who you are. No longer governed by stereotypes of what is good-looking, beauty today is not about being someone else; beauty is about your own personal appeal. "We don't want to look like anybody, we want other people to want to look like us." This is what one young girl had to say when asked about her beauty role model. When it comes to beauty, today's young women are their own role models. They want to maximize their own natural appeal.

It correlates that the dark skin taboo is, well, fading. Many of the top heroines in the Hindi cinema today are dusky. Choosing the term *dusky* over *dark* in itself reflects a mindset shift. Being dusky has become a part of the beauty code, whereas being dark has long been a huge social negative. Commenting on the change, a 24-year-old woman in Mumbai said, "Nowadays people with dark skin are called black beauty; earlier they were called *saanwali* [dark]." Bollywood heroines—still in many ways the yardstick for feminine beauty in India—exemplify this shift, as some of the more successful ones today—such as Bipasha Basu and Priyanka Chopra—are dusky, not fair.

If life is a theatre, then accessories are becoming the essential props. Highlighters (in hair or otherwise) are the accents that draw your attention where it is intended. You could call them "hot-spot pointers." Traditional *mehendi* has risen to the occasion in the form of the *mehendi* tattoo. Nose rings are no longer confined to the nose. The definition of beauty accessories has itself undergone a major change. Mobile phones and bikes are accessories too. They help you highlight yourself and enhance your appearance. As someone pointed out in one of the consumer interactions, "If I carry a good-looking mobile phone, I think I look better."

Aparna Agrawal, a fashion designer from Mumbai who sells her wares to upper-middle-class consumers, rightly puts it: "Beauty today is a combination of your personality, the way you look, the way you carry yourself, and the person you are, which comes out as being beautiful or not. Beauty is a package today. Awareness has definitely increased because of the exposure, and the fashion trends are easily accessible. So there is more scope for even average-looking people to look more beautiful. You can make someone look beautiful today."[5]

Engaging through the Body

Heroes with gym-sculpted bodies are on top of the Bollywood charts. Being shirtless on the screen now isn't a misdemeanor, but a delight and pleasure. Some heroes, such as John Abraham and Ranbir Kapor, have gone beyond just being shirtless. India has discovered the male cleavage. On *Koffee with Karan* (a chat show hosted by a celebrity director), Shahid Kapoor (an up-and-coming actor) was paired with Esha Deol (an up-and-coming actress);

a very normal pairing, except that Shahid's neckline plunged deeper than Esha's.

Today in India, skin is an important part of fashion. Exposed skin has become as normal in Indian lives as blue denim. On an everyday basis, we are exposed to a lot more skin on the TV, in our offices, or on the roads than we were a few years ago. The designer sketches are being penciled with skin as an important element of the apparel design. Cleavage today is displayed by men and women alike. A hint of cleavage is more a fashion state-ment than a mark of desperation as it was viewed earlier.

With the body finally getting its due in the beauty scheme of things, Vaseline has launched a body fairness lotion, Healthy White Body Milk, which claims to make your body as fair as your face. Body care rituals too are gaining favor. Hair removal and skin bleaching categories are seeing increased action by players such as Dabur (which has taken over Fem), Reckitt Benckiser (Veet), Gillette, and others. Body lotions in general are finding their legitimate share in the personal care segment in India.

Slimming as a market in India is gaining ground. According to an FICCI–Ernst and Young study of April 2009, the fitness cat-egory, including gyms and slimming centers, is expected to grow by more than 25 percent.[6] Vandana Luthra's Curls & Curves (VLCC), one of the pioneer players in the slimming space, today has a pan-India presence of nearly 225 outlets across 75 cities. With the idea of beauty now including the body, these consumer categories are set to grow exponentially.

The Connection between Health and Good Looks

Health in India has been very much a visual idea. Health and prosperity went hand in hand; wealth was displayed in an expanding girth. A rounded body and a chubby face were indi-cators of prosperous good health. But now the idea of health is changing, though the measure of it remains visual. Today the lean, chiseled body is emblematic of good health.

The rising health consciousness has had a profound impact on the idea of beauty and beauty products. The market for prod-ucts that merely work cosmetically to make you look good has dwindled. Today, products that make you look good must also do something good for your skin. Conversely, because health is expected to be visibly evident, even those products that are designed to do you good—for example, providing nourishment—must also make you look good.

The changing dynamic between health and looks has led to an interesting shift in the value propositions of various consumer products and brands. The inherently do-good brands, such as Parachute and Vatika hair oil, are each in their own way attempting to amplify the effects of well-nourished hair. Their advertising has highlighted the freedom that well-nourished hair gives you to color and style at your will, without worrying about the side effects. Dabur's Gulabari rosewater, which was known for its inherent do-goodness, now promises the effect of a rose-like glow. Even rural brands such as Dabur Lal Dant Manjan (toothpowder) have moved their platform from merely promising "problem-free teeth"; now the claim is "problem-free and therefore good-looking teeth." On a similar note, brands and products that stood for pure cosmetic appeal are claiming do-good benefits. Lakme's Radiance Complexion compact, essentially a face powder, has added Vitamin E and C to moisturize the skin and protect it from pollution.

In this two-way flow between health and looks, almost all Ayurveda and herbal brands have had to travel the distance from being merely about nourishment and health benefits to a promise of visual enhancement. Similarly, purely cosmetic brands have had to reengineer either the product or the brand to deliver on some do-good aspect. As a result, there is a convergence of propositions from both Ayurveda and cosmetic brands. Ayurveda brands, such as those of Dabur, are working harder to deliver on effectiveness variables, and cosmetic brands such as those of Hindustan Unilever are adding herbal ingredients to mitigate the harshness of cosmetic ingredients.

As a consequence, the market for purely surface-effect products has shrunk dramatically. For instance, the market share for soaps that promise only beauty or freshness, such as Rexona and Liril, has declined, while those touting health benefits leading to confidence or beauty, such as Lifebuoy or Medimix, are doing well.

Even the quintessential beauty soap of India, Lux, which is positioned as the beauty soap of the film stars, now offers variants with almonds, strawberry, peaches, and cream that promise softer and smoother skin.

Driven by a Larger Cultural Change

As we've seen, the Indian concept of beauty has shifted in many ways: from a focus on the face alone to embracing the appearance of the body as well, from being static and two-dimensional to being active and three-dimensional, from being held back to being vibrant, from a focus merely on attractiveness to a focus on health leading to good looks, from struggling to emulate a narrow ideal to making the most of your own unique appeal.

Driving this change is a larger cultural shift in the way we are living our lives today. As Indians, we have always lived through our minds. We have defined our identity through our relationships, found simplicity more seductive than success, and seen pleasure as an internal demon to be conquered. Liberalization has now lived for more than a decade in India. What was essentially an economic unshackling has also led to the opening up of our minds.

Indians are now learning to live through their bodies. There is more choreography in Bollywood song sequences today than facial expressions. The camera takes more long shots than close-ups. Editing has assumed paramount importance. The music itself has moved from melody to beats. Dance numbers have replaced dream sequences. Dance shows on TV are sharing the ratings with family dramas. The body, revealed in its full form, is center stage. On shows like *Khatron Ke Khiladi* (the Indian version of *Fear Factor*), models and actresses perform stunts that would challenge a professional stunt performer. Beauty in this frame is physical, clad in swimwear, and full of adventure.

Flipping the Beauty Equation

In the new construct of Indian beauty, because of the body being at the center stage, personality has also come to the fore. Looking good is a complete package: it includes the way you talk, the way you walk, and the way you carry yourself. Bad breath has beauty implications—it's not enough to have a shapely body if you have an unhealthy stomach. What looks good must be supported by inner beauty.

This has two major implications. First, the number of variables one can play with has suddenly increased. You may not have the shapeliest nose, but your gift of gab could probably compensate for it. Second, beauty is variable: it can be altered, enhanced, acquired, cultivated, and groomed. A trim figure can be maintained; accents can be acquired. You can have green eyes or purple or blue ones, depending on your mood that day; it's just a matter of buying lenses off the shelf.

The change has also made the inner-outer continuum smoother. Grooming is about your inner attitude, worn on your sleeve. If you are confident inside, you look good outside. This flow is not just from inside to outside—it works both ways. What you do outside makes you beautiful inside. A meaningful persona, doing good in the world, adds to your physical beauty and enhances it. Also, traditional stereotypes of fair skin, a sharp nose, and a long neck are no longer must-haves as beauty requirements. Bipasha Basu (a popular Indian actress) has dusky skin; she is no longer called *saanwali* (dark). The changing archetype is exemplified by the changing image of the airhostess, from the demure and self-contained *sari*-clad woman of Indian Airlines to the more flamboyant and stylish, skirt-wearing girl of Kingfisher Airlines.

The Indian Beauty Market

The space for beauty brands in India is polarized. At one end, the market is getting more and more specific and specialized, with claims such as "reduced hair breakage from the first wash" and "two tones fairer skin in just seven days." At the other end, consumers are still buying larger-than-life transformation stories: the protagonist in the Fair & Lovely story becoming a commentator, the Pond's White Beauty story of winning back a lost love. It's important to understand that some of the personal care categories, such as soaps and creams, have become static, with little innovation and excitement. To be able to capture the consumer's imagination, their ordinariness therefore requires them to tell stories that are larger than life, almost Bollywood-like.

Although at the proposition end there is a polarization, at the benefits end there is a convergence—a merger of benefits across categories. For instance, nourishment, which was formerly strictly a hair oil proposition, has entered the language of shampoos in a big way. Lipsticks are offering moisturizing; fairness comes forti-fied with sunscreen. In many cases, what was almost a detractor for the category has become an attractor: for example, hair oils touted as "light" (formerly heavy), herbal bleach (formerly harsh chemicals), and hair-protecting colorants (once damaging).

Continuing the pattern of do-good in everything, specialist products are being promoted for everyday use. Clinic All Clear dandruff shampoo is being promoted for everyday use. Pepsodent claims to have Germicheck, protecting your teeth on a 24-hour basis. Daily usage creams include sunscreen. Products once focused for specialized fairness and age-defying regimens are fighting for a share of the consumer's everyday beauty routine.

Another new trend is that of traditional products embracing science, which means traditional ingredients and recipes are being rendered in scientific packaging. Cucumber extracts and milk pro-tein system are examples. At the same time, the process behind natural ingredients is being played up for its efficacy—whether it's Vatika, going to great lengths to explain the role of its key ingredient amla in strengthening hair roots, or Nyle, which extols the role of soya and almonds in its hair-strengthening shampoo.

Also shaping up is the market for good looks for men. A Gillette India study of early 2008 indicated that men now spend an average of 20 minutes in front of the mirror each morning, longer than the 18-minute average for Indian women.[7] Emami's Fair & Handsome fairness cream for men has already posted sales of more than $11 million in the one and a half years since its launch. Garnier has launched Garnier MEN, a new range of products designed specifically for men. Incidentally, India was the first country where Garnier launched this line. One of its first launches is the lightening cream for men in the men's fairness market, which is estimated at Rs.175 *crores* (nearly $40 million) and is growing at the rate of 25 percent annually.[8]

The entire men's grooming market in India is currently estimated at Rs.1500 *crores* ($310 million), and is growing at a 12 percent compounded annual growth rate (CAGR).[9]

An Instrument for Life Fulfillment

Beauty today is not an end in itself; it's a means to larger ends. It has transactional value in life. It can make things happen. It can bring you fulfillment. Seeking a transformation in the way you look is a clear consequence of this change. The desire is to bring out the best of what we have inside us. And a lot of this is attitude driven rather than destiny driven.

India today is at its fertile best in terms of opportunities, ambitions, and people's desire to transform their own destinies. In this quest, Indians need props that can help them get to their goal better and faster. Beauty and the way you present yourself to the larger world through your personality, grooming, and mannerisms is fast becoming the ladder that Indians are using to reach their destiny. How you look is of increasing importance, especially in areas where it formerly mattered little. A job interview has always been a test of knowledge and mental prowess, but today your X Factor can make the difference. This is a turning point in the Indian mindset.

Brands in the space of beauty, grooming, and fashion therefore need to be at the leading edge of this change, driving it rather than following it. The business and marketing implications of this larger sociocultural change are not difficult to see. For starters, with so much skin now exposed, we can expect almost a revolution in the range of skin-care products and services. From the facially focused beauty care range of products, we need to expand into a more holistic and coordinated body care range of products and services.

For most beauty brands, the easier route has always been to promise the consumer a transformation: the chance to become somebody else. Brands have made fortunes establishing and selling stereotypes of beauty. There is much to be learned from the roadside retailers of fashion accessories on Linking Road in Mumbai, or Sarojini Nagar in Delhi. There the entire business model is around mix-and-match separates and dresses and using accessories to help the customer create the best look for herself, rather than selling a stereotypical look. The challenge for today's brands and products is to help customers highlight their natural appeal. Is there a market, perhaps, for a body lotion that brings out the best in the darker Indian skin tones?

Indians are realizing the value of beauty as an instrument for life fulfillment, as something that you can manipulate, use, and ride on, for success as well as pleasure. Beauty today is about confidence, about success and living life to the fullest—not just keeping the opposite sex engaged. Beauty today is about the body. And our body is our representational currency in this world; the username that we log on to the world with, and the profile under which we play. This has implications not just on the portrayal of beauty in advertising, but also on real products and services and their specific deliveries. If beauty is playing a larger role in the lives of the people, our products, brands, and services in this category must do so as well.

4

MASALA MEDIA

ENTERTAINMENT FOR THE TASTE BUDS

Rationed Entertainment

Until around the 1990s, entertainment and leisure, like most other things in India, had long been a subject of control and rationing. The Indian censorship board built a reputation for being as tough and calculating in choosing what content may pass through its screen as the Ministry of External Affairs is when it comes to crafting joint statements between India and Pakistan. Before television, cinema was long the staple entertainment, complemented in part by the radio. There were times when Indians, as one, were riveted to their radio sets for *Binaca Geetmala*, a weekly radio countdown show of top songs from Indian cinema. The show's host, Ameen Sayani, became a household name—and Radio Ceylon, which aired the show, was a favorite frequency. But Indians got this entertainment only in permitted doses, similar to their food allowances on their ration cards.

Entertainment in India traditionally has been treated as a nutritional substance to be doled out as if by parents (who know best) to children (who need to be protected from their own appetites). Most channels, like radio and television, were run by the government, and cinema was censored by a board controlled by the Ministry of Information and Broadcasting. As a result, average middle-class Indians—who slogged through the day in government jobs or their own businesses so they could afford a television set—came home to watch *Krishi Darshan* (an educational program on agriculture). Television programming followed the government's agenda of driving national integration and population control and of promoting scientific agriculture, with only a reluctant acceptance of the need for pure entertainment. This was addressed with a 15-minute slot on Wednesdays in the program called *Chitrahaar*—a collection of songs from Bollywood—and a two-and-a-half hour slot on Sundays for a Bollywood movie. Every week these two programs united the television audience, holding families and their neighbors captive in front of their TV sets. There was a high element of suspense, as most of the time viewers didn't even know which movie or what kind of songs would be screened.

In the early days after independence, even Bollywood storylines were built around the themes of national pride and the increasing rural/urban divide. Movies such as *Naya Daur*, a blockbuster in 1957, were set in post-independence India, where industrialization was slowly creeping in, displacing traditional livelihoods. In time, however, cinema moved on from nationalist themes to the angst of Indian youth and their futile struggle against the system. Amitabh Bachchan, as an angry Vijay, gave voice to this feeling of frustration and helplessness. In the late 1980s, Bollywood recognized sexual repression as the single greatest issue of the day, and deep pelvic thrusts accompanied by heaving bosoms entered the language of Indian cinema. The entertainment code in India had evolved, from being about pure nutrition to expressing angst and a deep-seated sexual repression.

The year 1990 marked the beginning of a media and entertainment revolution in India. The impetus came with the advent of the first Gulf war. CNN's beamed news reports of the bombing of Kuwait by Saddam Hussein sparked a huge demand for satellite dishes. The launch of Star TV and Zee TV, close on the heels of this event, further fuelled the spread of cable television in India. From a modest beginning of 412, 000 households in the first half of 1992, coverage grew to 95 million cable and satellite TV households in India in 2009, with 16 million private direct to home (DTH) subscribers.[1] The media and entertainment industry in India today is poised to boom. According to a

PricewaterhouseCoopers forecast, the industry is set to grow by 10.5 percent cumulatively over 2009–2013 to reach Rs.92,900 *crores* ($19 billion).[2]

The Changing Conscience of the Nation

Media in India—especially national television, and to a large extent the cinema too—has become the screen of India's conscience. Government regulations determined what was fit to be shown to the general masses and thus heavily influenced what was socially acceptable and what wasn't. Post-independence, storylines pandered to the strong nationalist feelings; through the 1980s they gave vent to frustrations. Doordarshan (the national channel run by the government) took it upon itself to tell the tales of the *Ramayana* and *Mahabharata*; Bollywood reiterated the themes of good conquering evil, love as a weapon against hatred, and the sanctity of the Indian family system. Morality in India had become a preserve of the celluloid.

Because TV and cinema had come to constitute the moral voice of the nation, it was expected that any change in the mindset and worldview would be reflected on these screens first—and it surely was. The joys of a new way of life, the loosening of social shackles, and the march toward freedom and modernity (with the old still firmly in tow) came to be the spirit of the 1990s. Bollywood found new sensibilities under directors such as David Dhawan, who ushered in an era of mindless fun strung together with purposeless storylines; at the other end of the spectrum, Karan Johar celebrated our newfound affluence and presented the joy of families in fluorescent colors and a new international scope.

Dhawan, who managed a series of hits back to back, became famous for his celebration of senselessness. His movies—*Coolie No.1* ("Porter No. 1"), *Biwi No. 1* ("Wife No. 1"), *Jodi No.1* ("Couple No. 1"), and so on—reveled in inane fun. The storylines were thin, the music was tailored to be popular, and the lyrics compensated for their lack of poetry with licentiousness. Bollywood actor Govinda, who almost single-handedly championed this breakthrough, wore bright fluorescent trousers with contrasting shirts and invented dance movements that highlighted the genre of nonsense. His antics became a topic of some cool conversations in swank social circles. Indian cinema, so long burdened with angst and repression, was shedding its heaviness and embracing fun. Comedy, which previously had served only as a brief reprieve from the high-voltage emotional drama in Indian films, had finally arrived as a genre. This was a first in the history of Bollywood, as there were no comedians in these movies—the hero himself played that role.

Karan Johar, on the other hand, was busy weaving tales of chiffon romance. Karan's was a world of pampered living, where personal helicopters were used as the vehicle of transport, money never stood in the way of relationships, and dads shook a leg, with the son and the daughter-in-law and other pretty dancers in tow. There was nothing subtle or low-key in this world; every emotion and celebration hit a high note. The film ended in everybody finding their true love and the audience happy with its journey to the land of candy floss and bubblegum romance.

With the opening of the airwaves and the entry of newer international and Indian channels on the local television, small-screen content also was opening up. Pleasure and entertainment, hitherto regulated and rationed, seemed to gain legitimacy and approval. The screen that reflected the moral code of the nation was maturing—and less reluctant to feature content with no perceived nutritional value. In some ways the changeover went too far, as if compensating for the many years of denial. Not that everything was being thrown out of the window, though; while the boundaries of pleasure and entertainment were being expanded, there still was a self-regulating conscience in place. The cultural arbiters were becoming more broadminded, but they were not about to be cast aside. As a result, despite the emergence of just-for-the-fun-of-it sheer entertainment, sexual undertones were still considered something that needed to be carefully managed.

Nothing Nutritional About It

Credit for opening up the television consciousness of India goes to a sudden mushrooming of music videos in early 2000. These music videos were among the first on the small screen to give India a dose of pure taste bud entertainment. For a country and its people brought up on the staple diet of mythological serials and family dramas such as *Buniyaad* ("Foundations")—an Indian television drama-series that dealt with the Partition of India and its aftermath—the music videos of this age were a revelation quite literally.

These music videos took old popular Bollywood numbers such as *Kaanta Laga* ("I've Been Pricked") and filmed them with girls in short skirts, with the dance form focusing on various kinds of pelvic thrusts. Whether it was the G-string of *Kaanta Laga*, the under-skirt shots of *Pyaari Bindu*, or the deliberate gestures of *Crazy Berry*, collectively the music videos expanded the boundaries of what television content Indians were willing to allow into their living rooms. No other art form to that point had been able to put the G-string at the center of a nationwide debate, making it okay for the intelligentsia to discuss the impact of a certain type of undergarment. While her music video expanded the boundary of social control, Shefali Zariwala, who played the DJ Doll in *Kaanta Laga*, shot to fame from nowhere and became a popular invitee at various shows and functions.

The most revealing aspect of these music videos, however, was their lack of interest in the actual music. They seemed to value the beat over singing ability, rhythm over lyrics, choreography over the narratives, and models over actors. In the pursuit of pure sensory pleasure, what appealed to the senses was more important than what appealed, say, to the soul. Music in these music videos was just an excuse for attaching some tasty visuals and maybe adding to the candy appeal of the whole package. Most videos therefore used a hit number from yesterday, thereby ensuring that the song was likeable, leaving only the visual part to be worked on. The use of old songs served another purpose, rather quietly but effectively: their presence was like permission from yesterday for the licentiousness of today.

The rise of taste bud entertainment has also meant groundbreaking success for movies such as *Om Shanti Om*, which is actually a remake of an old and successful Bollywood story of reincarnation, spiced up with all the Bollywood *masala* available in the recipe book. The movie is in many ways a parody as well as a tribute to typical Bollywood. To its credit, more than 42 well-known Bollywood stars appear in the course of the film, including thirty of them in one song alone. *Om Shanti Om* grossed around $39 million worldwide, becoming the second-highest-grossing Hindi movie at its time of release. As a movie, it was the epitome of slick, surface entertainment; certainly tangy on the tongue, and if it didn't stir the soul, so what?

Entertainment in today's India has successfully extricated itself from the clutches of the nutritional imperative. The small screen and the large screen both are liberated from the burden of presenting a moral at the end of the story. What titillates is what's being sold: nothing less, nothing more. Unlike what the moral pundits of society might have to say about this, there are distinct advantages to this unburdening. The biggest one is that the distinction between art and commercial cinema has started to crumble. According to the earlier distinction, whatever belonged to the realm of reality was relegated to the world of art cinema. Art almost came to be an excuse for cinema that was not entertaining and had little to offer to the audience. In the new context, however, there are enough examples of directors treating real subjects in a way that connects with the audience as a piece of entertainment, not only winning praise from the critics. *Life in a Metro*, for example—whose narrative interweaves the lives of seven people living in Mumbai, exploring issues such as extramarital affairs and the sanctity of love and marriage—is one of many recent Indian movies that are both true-to-life and commercially successful. Art need not be divorced from being commercial anymore.

Reel Life Meets Real Life

Historically, reality in India has been something from which to escape. There is nothing really to celebrate in a life full of disappointments, struggle, and sacrifices. The exception to this—the smaller joys of being together and the strength of family ties—was a staple of Indian cinema and television content for many years. Apart from this aspect of real life, however, entertainment content in India was always about an escape, either to a land of love and romance where this emotion was not shackled by the society or to a plane of action where life's wrongs were avenged. Reality and any reflection of it was best avoided; it was unfertile ground for entertainment.

In today's entertainment content, however, real life has infected reel lives like never before. The narratives and characters are becoming much closer to what's really happening in people's lives. The trend toward relatively more realistic cinema started with *Dil Chahta Hai* ("The Heart Desires" or "Do Your Thing"), released in 2001. The movie was set in modern-day urban Mumbai and told the story of three young friends. The trend was reaffirmed with *Rang De Basanti* ("Paint It Saffron"), released in 2006. The movie sought to connect with the burning desire of today's youth to go out and make a difference. Set against the backdrop of a documentary on India's freedom struggle being made by a British filmmaker, the movie dealt with some stark issues of political corruption affecting the lives of the armed forces.

Today's entertainment in India has shifted from the earlier themes of fighting crime and poverty, avenging a sister's rape and a family's honor; today's cinema is built more around friendships, live-in relationships, and everyday heroes. Storylines are more focused, with a clear targeting of a specific audience and its mindset. Movies that try to pack in something for everybody are on the decline. Stories of interpersonal relationships and regular people pushing beyond their limits are on the upswing.

Change is apparent in what's being spoken on screen. The earlier movies' dialog was hyperbolic, more like exchanges of slogans than conversations. The dialog in today's films is truer to the interactions between characters in the scene, not trying so hard to deliver a punch for the audience. The newer cinema language is experimenting with everything from obscenities to slang. *Omkara*, an adaptation of Shakespeare's *Othello* released in 2006, was probably the first mainstream Hindi movie liberally peppered with the swear words that had been generally absent from mainstream Indian cinema. The fact that the movie grossed more than $16 million worldwide is proof of its wide acceptance.

The earlier version of the Indian film hero was absolute in his goodness and morality, while the villain embodied all the negatives. Increasingly, the characters in Indian cinema are no longer so black and white, but depicted in shades of gray. Most storylines today don't even have a separate villain. Quite often, the hero himself has a negative side to his character. Rather than fighting a villain, the hero today needs to prevail over circumstances or fight his own demons. Take, for example, a movie like *Dev D*, a modern take on the classic novel *Devdas*, which has been rendered for the Indian screen nine times already. In its classical form, *Devdas* is a story of self-destruction by the protagonist for want of love and care. *Dev D* has been applauded for being groundbreaking and adventurous in its reinterpretation of the classic. Unlike the original, in this adapted version the protagonist, rather than fully destroying himself, is actually able to face his internal demons and return to the woman he thinks he loves. This is a completely new resolution of a time-honored classic, more true to the current times.

A big shift toward reality has also taken place in the portrayal of women. Screen mothers today are much more modern and rather broadminded. In *Dilwale Dulhania Le Jayenge* ("The Lover Will Take the Bride"), released in 1995, the mother of the female protagonist, played by Farida Jalal, exhorts her to dream but not expect her dreams to be fulfilled. In *Hum Tum* ("Me and You"), released some nine years later, Kirron Kher plays a mother who exhorts her daughter to not only dream freely but also go ahead and fulfill those dreams. The typical mother of the Bollywood movies is no longer a slave to the sewing machine; she is the progressive modern woman who stands up to the wrong and encourages the right.

The character of female protagonists is changing too. In *Biwi No. 1* ("Wife No. 1"), released in 1999, Karishma Kapoor played a doting and dutiful wife; in *Dhoom 2*, released in 2006, Aishwarya Rai plays a crime partner to her love interest, played by Hrithik Roshan. Women protagonists in most of the cinema now are getting equitable if not larger roles. Moreover, there is a considerable increase in the number of movies with women as the focus of their storyline. Movies like *Fashion*, *Page 3*, and *Dor* ("String"), for instance, were built around women and did reasonably well at the box office.

The Reality of Television

The distance between reel and reality is fast vanishing on television as well. Reality shows have gone beyond talent shows to weight-loss competitions and the art of surviving in a jungle. It all started with *Kaun Banega Crorepati* (India's *Who Wants to Be a Millionaire?*), which transformed the fortunes of both the Star TV network and actor Amitabh Bachchan. *Indian Idol* (based on *American Idol*) did the same for Sony Entertainment Television. Colors defied all the rules for a general entertainment channel by launching with a reality show called *Khatron Ke Khiladi* (based on *Fear Factor*), which reached the top slot on the television rating points (TRPs), elbowing aside many established players.

News channels, too, seem bent on becoming reality shows—and why wouldn't they? After all, reality is their rightful business. Newsrooms now host, in detail, real-life dramas like "six-year-old boy Aniket kidnapped and killed by servant" or "daughter of rickshaw driver tops school with 95 percent score." Stories like these—which may have high drama value but little social, political, or economic significance—command a lot of air time on news channels and are analyzed by experts for hours. The adage that news should be as local as possible seems to have given news channels a definitive idea of how to shore up the TRPs.

Soaps on Indian television had until recently made a meal of celebrating large extended families and their internal upheavals. Sibling rivalries, births out of wedlock, husbands going astray had been their staples. Of late, however, they too seem to be moving beyond the old formula. The focus in some of the newly launched soaps is more on the individual than on the family. Serials like *Bhaskar Bharti*, *Palampur Express*, and *Ladies Special* all base their storylines on ordinary individuals and their personal journeys. There seems to be an end to the saga of *saas-bahu* (the rivalry between daughter-in-law and mother-in-law) that dominated the Indian television for most of the first decade of the twenty-first-century.

The Indian television scene, however, is a medley of various kinds of narratives. On the one hand there is programming, such as *MTV Splitsvilla* that targets the youth, with dialog that's punctuated by beeps (read: obscenities) and incidents that will shock any middle-class parent. On the other hand is a program like *Khatron Ke Khiladi*, that is trying to position itself for the family audience. *Khatron Ke Khiladi* attempts to balance close-ups of bikini-clad women with the *Gayatri Mantra*—a Hindu recital for auspicious beginnings. Both of these programs coexist on television today, as both reflect a part of India's current reality.

The Bollywood of earlier days was another world in the fantasies it would weave and the lives its stars would live. The fact that it was so distant from the common person in its content and positioning added to the allure of Bollywood. Television, in contrast, seems to be making stardom an equal-opportunity proposition. Multiple reality shows across channels are giving birth to mini stars every day. Today anyone with a bit of talent and a little perseverance has a fair chance at stardom if only for a few episodes. The popularity of reality television seems to suggest that Indians today prefer watching the likes of themselves becoming stars to viewing the faraway stars of Tinseltown.

Pleasure, Purpose, and Platform

There are three key pillars emerging for media brands to be built on. The first and foremost is *pleasure*, which today is a must deliverable, irrespective of the medium and the genre. Entertainment is no longer the sole jurisdiction of entertainment channels or cinema. News has to be entertainment as well. Page 3 in the *Times of India* (India's largest national daily), which carries news of the city socialites and their parties, is a much-read and discussed section that has even inspired a movie by the same name. There is a blurring of the lines: content that seems to belong to an entertainment channel is being featured on a news channel and vice versa.

The second pillar for media brands comes from their ability to activate mass momentum. The biggest glitch in the India growth story has been a failure of the infrastructure and civic support systems. There has been a big gap between the progress of Indians and the progress of India. Media in the past few years seems to have taken up this *purpose* and have played a key role in many instances. One such example is the city of Mumbai, which has been under continuous threat in the past few years. The maximum city, as it is called, was fully submerged by heavy rains in 2005 and then was ripped apart by serial bomb blasts in trains in 2006. The most nerve-racking experience was in 2009, when multiple locations—including two high-end hotels—came under deadly siege by terrorists.

Each time the city of Mumbai has been hit by the fury of nature or terrorists, the civic and police infrastructures have given way. And each time, the media have done the job of rallying the citizens, giving voice to their frustrations and grievances and calling out the authorities in question. After the Mumbai floods, the *Times of India* actually mounted a huge petition, which its readers could sign through email or SMS. After the 2009 terrorist attack on Mumbai, some of the biggest protest rallies were organized and supported by news channels such as CNN-IBN and NDTV 24x7. There are examples from across the nation proving the media's ability to catalyze mass opinion. The Jessica Lall murder case of 1999 is a prime example of effective media activism. The case was appealed because the media stood up to question the verdict—the acquittal of her accused killer, Manu Sharma—which public opinion overwhelmingly saw as a miscarriage of justice. (Judgment on the appeal convicted Sharma and sentenced him to life in prison.)

The media have finally discovered their unique power in the world's largest democracy. If legislature, executive, and judiciary are meant to be the three key pillars of the Indian governmental system, then the media are fast emerging as the fourth pillar. The media's ability to rally people and build opinion has resulted in actions that would not otherwise have come about. The big difference, however, is not that the media are playing a role in airing people's views, but that they are actively building momentum that leads to action.

Television has emerged as one of the biggest *platforms* for showcasing talent. Until recently there were only two ways to find an opportunity in Bollywood: either you were born into a Bollywood family or you had to run away to Mumbai in the hope of finding a place in Indian cinema. Bollywood is full of stories of the struggles that many actors and actresses have gone through to get a chance to showcase their talent. Television talent shows have taken the opportunity stage from Mumbai to smaller cities and towns. Aspirants no longer have to run off to Mumbai; the kingmakers of Bollywood are fanning out to other locales, conducting auditions to find the hottest talent in music and dancing. There is no denying that reality television is nothing but the game of TRPs. But what's also undeniable is the media's role in bringing out talents who would otherwise have struggled on the streets of Mumbai.

Lead India was an initiative that combined both purpose and platform in one television program. The program was launched on India's sixtieth Independence Day by the *Times of India* to select a new leader for the country. Lead India gave a platform to people who had the ability and the desire to make a difference to India's public governance but did not want to go through the mess of politics. The fame and the resources that this program brought to its winners helped them shorten the frustrating and uncertain path up the political ladder. The initiative, however, went beyond just selecting a candidate; it actually took up the cause of voting in a big way during the 2009 elections. Had it not been for the backing of one of the largest media houses in the country, Lead India wouldn't have been the success that it was.

Pleasure, purpose, and platform are no longer optional roles for media brands in India to play. Every media brand, whether it's in the space of radio or television or cinema, needs to have a combination of these three attributes. Media and the entertainment business no longer operate in a one-way flow; it's two-way now, entertaining and being entertained in return. It's not just about passive broadcasting but also about actively championing what matters to people's lives. All this not with any dose of heaviness; media today must appeal to our senses and our sense, no matter what the medium.

From Broadcast to Narrowcast

The entertainment and media arena is slowly but certainly becoming segmented. These are definitely not the times of one size fits all. Bollywood, for example, is witnessing the rising phenomenon of multiplex movies, cinema made for the multiplex audiences who are urban and relatively more discerning than the average masses. Movies such as *Bheja Fry*, *Life in a Metro*, *Page 3*, *Corporate*, and *Traffic Signal*—each made with a budget of anywhere from Rs.6 to Rs.40 million, fairly modest by Bollywood standards—have managed to recoup up to four times their cost at the box office. The economics of multiplex movies have started to make sense because finally there is an audience willing to shell out Rs. 150–200 to watch a film with a slightly different take. The fact that multiplex theatres have a smaller capacity per screen to fill has also helped justify the equation.

The other space where narrowcasting is becoming increasingly important is that of news. With increasing localization of coverage and rising literacy levels, Hindi news as a segment is growing. In print, for instance, Hindi newspapers have the highest growth rate. *Dainik Jagran* and *Dainik Bhaskar* not only top the list of Hindi dailies but are also the top two dailies in the country, according to the *Indian Readership Survey 2010*.[3] A Hindi daily like *Dainik Jagran*, for instance, prints at 30 locations in 11 states and ends up producing 204 subeditions. Certainly these regional language dailies are closer to the ground and to the hearts of their readers and thus are building a viable regional news segment.

The divide between the English and the Hindi world continues in the television news space as well. The difference between English and Hindi news channels is as much in their content as in their language. What makes headlines at the top English news channels is quite different from what makes headlines on Hindi news. Hindi news channels are skewed toward stories of human interest, entertainment, and sensational crimes. Stories such as "*Mandir ka rahasya*," a mystery feature of children who visited a temple and never wanted to return to their parents, or "*Yamraj se mulakat*," in which a dead man comes back to life and recounts his experiences after death, are staples on many Hindi news channels. The English news channels, on the other hand, are obsessed with national politics and the degradation of civil society. What works for the Hindi audience in this case appears to be different from what works for the English-speaking audience. This underlines the need for news providers to tailor their coverage to the specific audience rather than aim for a broad national audience.

The trend of narrowcasting is also significant when it comes to magazines. While mainstream magazines are losing readership at a steady pace, there are significant activities in the specialist or niche magazine space. From mid-2007 to 2008, there were at least 20 such titles launched, according to the *This Year, Next Year* report by Group M.[4] Leading magazine publishing houses like the Worldwide Media and India Today groups have entered into partnerships to bring many international brands to India. Within a span of a year or so, India has added to its magazine stands brands like *GQ*, *Vogue*, *Rolling Stone*, and *Forbes*, to name just a few. Clearly, niche offerings are beginning to be profitable in the space of entertainment and media. India is a country of many diverse audiences, and the media needs to move from broadcast to narrowcast.

Media in Different SKUs

Just like personal care products, entertainment also needs to be available in various sizes. The game of cricket, for example, once at least an all-day tournament, now can be played and viewed as a three-and-a-half-hour match, running just a bit longer than a typical movie. This new form of cricket, also called Twenty20 or T20, packs a lot more adrenaline into a much shorter time frame. The packaging of the game itself has borrowed freely from soccer codes. Cheerleaders have been brought in, and their Lycra-clad bodies move to drumbeats whenever the ball hits the boundary. T20 is the new SKU (stock keeping unit) of cricket entertainment.

The news, too, needs to be made available in different sizes to meet the access preferences of different viewers. People today don't care so much whether they see it on television or read it in the newspaper—what matters is that they get just the bit of news they want when they really want it. People with less time may want to know just the breaking news; for them, an SMS update or a website that's easily accessible works well. When they have more time, they may seek a slightly deeper analysis—then a television feature or a newspaper article will have more appeal. At yet another time they may want online access to a favorite TV program, because they missed it the previous evening or they want to forward a link to a friend. In the world of increasing information parity, it's the access that's driving our media choices. People are pulling out what interests them when and where they can. Media brands need to see themselves as portals of content available in various SKUs and across media, not as solely a television or a print player.

The biggest driver that's forcing providers to offer bite-sized content is the mobile phone. The device is fast replacing the camera and the music player and soon could be the most preferred screen. With over 427 million subscribers in India, the mobile phone is already the country's single most popular music device. For Bharti Airtel, India's largest mobile service provider, over 30 percent of revenues from value added services (VAS) comes from music, as reported by the *Economic Times* in August 2009.[5] As entertainment goes portable, content will have to follow suit. UTV, a leading media and entertainment company in India, has struck a deal with Sony Ericsson to offer four blockbuster movies on memory cards embedded in the handsets. This licensing deal for four of its films—*Jodhaa Akbar, Rang De Basanti, Race*, and *Fashion*—has netted UTV Rs.10 million and a completely new audience segment.

Reflecting Change, Driving Change

The media for the new emerging India have been both a mirror of change and a catalyst of change. In the desire to stay ahead and stay fresh, media have woven narratives that show India what it can become. Movies like *Chak De! India* and reality shows like *Indian Idol* have presented an image of a progressive India, moving ahead. By providing platforms for people to showcase themselves, by championing the purpose of effective public governance, the media have played a definitive role in catalyzing India's ambitions.

In this journey of change, however, media that had become the screen of India's social conscience have undergone their own changes. Entertainment content today can get away with a lot, including a movie that generates humor with its gay theme (*Dostana*) and another that explores the tensile strength in relationships of love and marriage (*Life in a Metro*). They have managed this without overtly crossing the line of culturally sanctioned subjects. Though media may be bursting the old boundaries on issues like morality, the industry has managed to keep the fabric of its own conscience relatively intact.

Television has learned from cinema; with its recent content, too, it pushes the boundaries time and again. It has realized that genres in entertainment are fluid. Reality television can be used to launch a general entertainment channel, which happened in the successful case of Colors. That genres can be blurred is the truth that news channels live every day, walking the tightrope between news and entertainment—and sometimes falling off when neighborhood gossip becomes "breaking news." Nevertheless, their genre has played a pivotal role in creating a public space in which citizens have come together for a cause, giving media a quasi-role in the governance scheme of things.

No other category resonates so closely with the changing culture and consumer, simultaneously leading and reflecting change. There are therefore no fixed formulas in the media category. Risks and adventures have generally been rewarded by the consumer. A portion of reality mixed with a portion of creativity has served as a good recipe to this point. But as newer forms of delivery take over—chiefly as the mobile phone becomes a key screen for infotainment—life will change yet again. What will not change is the fact that media will always be both the leading indicator and the creator of this change.

MEANINGFUL TECHNOLOGY

THE CULTURAL CIRCUITRY OF TECHNOLOGY PRODUCTS

It's Not about Efficiency

Most Indians don't want to understand technology. They need technology to understand them. We find evidence of this on the reality television show *Kaun Banega Crorepati* (*Who Wants to Be a Millionaire?*), in a particular phrase that its anchor, Amitabh Bachchan, used every time he had to record the final answer—"*Computerji lock kiya jaaye*" (Computer, lock in the final answer"). *Ji* in India is a suffix of respect. Thanks to this conferred title, a box of cold technology took on a character of authority and respect. *Computerji* became an unbiased referee, receptacle of much wisdom, who needed to be addressed with words of endearment. Thus the term *computerji* served two very critical functions required for the credibility of a show like this. If it weren't a computer, it wouldn't be impartial; and if it didn't come with honorific "*ji*," it wouldn't get the respect of an authority.

Computerji as a nomenclature embodies exactly how Indians use technology, putting it to the use that we deem it fit for rather than necessarily what it is designed for. There are many celebrated examples: using the washing machine for churning *lassi* (a refreshing drink made by churning curd) or using the engine made for farm equipment to power a manual cart (popularly called *Maruta*) or even using a hair dryer as a packaging tool to shrink-wrap items in plastic. These examples are generally celebrated as a testimony to Indian ingenuity. However, they prove something bigger: in India, technology has to fit into our lives in the way we need it; we do not want to have to change our lives to meet the demands of technology.

Consider the computer, for instance. It is essentially an efficiency device. Its greatest merit lies in being able to process large amounts of data at high speeds. For the mainstream Indian, however, the computer is meaningful for its ability to reduce human bias and subjective judgments. Some of the most popular uses of the computer—for "computerized horoscopes," "computerized eye testing," or "computerized lottery"—are clearly about removing human bias and achieving higher levels of accuracy. India, the largest democracy in the world, has now adopted electronic voting machines (EVMs) for its general elections. The central appeal of EVMs is not the fact that they eliminate the tedious process of manually counting so many votes, but the fact that they eliminate the chances of voter fraud. EVMs as machines are unbiased watchdogs, unlike the officers in the state machinery, who are ultimately human and prone to biases.

In a country with an abundance of human resources, the idea of computer as an efficiency driver actually met with resistance at first. Opposition parties protested that computerization would lead to unemployment. Obviously they didn't imagine that one day this machine would turn India into the biggest back office of the world—and generate unprecedented employment. From their point of view, the computer technology by itself was unfathomable, hence they rejected it. However, as the gateway to a career in IT the computer quickly became a much desired machine. Computer courses of all types and sizes now are being taught from large cities to small towns. In most Indian homes today the computer enters as an enabler of knowledge rather than a technological tool. Just as traditional Indian households brought in the *Encyclopedia Britannica* and *Reader's Digest* as references of knowledge, today's families are bringing home a computer.

Social Leapfrogging

The computer has been accepted in India not because it makes our work easy but because it gives us access to a whole new world of career opportunities. An education in IT today has become synonymous with a global career, which can turn a middle-class Indian who may not ever have traveled out of his own state before into a globetrotter. If Indians today are queuing up to study computers and information technology as a subject, it's thanks to this allure of a career that will help them escape their middle-class status, not because they fancy the technology for its own sake.

As with the computer, the mobile phone in India has not followed the typical technology adoption curve of other countries. In fact, even as the number of telephone connections surpassed 464.82 million in early 2009, fixed-line subscribers stayed at just 37.53 million. The mobile phone in India is thus not an upgrade in addition to the landline; rather, for a large part of the population it's their first experience of a personal telephone. Thus for most of India the cell phone is the only way they have experienced a telephone, free and untethered. In fact, the landline phone remained a luxury item throughout the 80s. Phones and cars belonged to the same social strata and were markers of a premium lifestyle. The mobile phone, on the other hand, seems to be fast becoming more of a necessity than a lifestyle choice. With rural India at 100 million mobile phone users and most of the growth in subscriptions coming from the bottom of the pyramid, the mobile phone is no longer a luxury purchase.

The value of the mobile phone for the majority of Indians is in the doors of opportunity it's opening. It's the mobile phone's ability to multiply potential that has led to the sudden boom and adoption of the technology in India, not the technological wow that it's a phone that operates without a cord. For the population engaged in everyday contract jobs of an electrician or a plumber or even a vegetable vendor, the mobile number has become a one-stop-shop. It has freed them from the need to rent a physical space or be tied to a particular location for business. For the rural population, it is their "lifeline," as promoted by Nokia, for emergencies or otherwise, when they need to connect to their loved ones and there are no other means available.

The mobile handset and service players as well as independent VAS operators have realized this. Their suite of services, especially for the rural consumer, is focused on this space of productivity enhancement. Thomson Reuters currently runs updates on the latest market trends, weather forecast, and crop information via its SMS-based service, which reaches some hundred thousand farmers as of this writing. Tata Indicom has just inaugurated a project in Gujarat that allows farmers to operate their irrigation pumps from remote locations without having to go to the farm. Similarly, Nokia has launched Life Tools Services, which offers agricultural and educational information to its customers.

The other important facet of technology in India is the social side of it. Moving up the social strata and gaining access to life at the next level are near-universal goals, now fulfilled by technology. The technology you own is a strong marker of your social standing. For instance, until air conditioners became rather commonplace, they were a huge status symbol. Gradually, even the desert coolers morphed their designs to look like the air conditioners. One of the popular desert cooler brands even advertised itself on the premise that it looked like an AC. The ad showed a jealous neighbor asking *"Suna hai tumne AC kharida hai?"* ("What's this I hear, you've bought an AC?"). Electronic home appliances like microwave ovens are still bought largely as status symbols in many Indian households. Most are used solely for reheating food just before a meal. Mobile phones too have come to be strongly associated with making a social statement. At the peak of the telecom boom, the average handset replacement cycle in India was down to 18 months. Sporting the latest model was much more important than the range of additional features.

The Indian mindset places a huge premium on the "latest" technology—perhaps because for so long this market has had to live with old and dated models. Until the markets of the emerging economies caught the fancy of global brands, markets like India's had to make do with old models in almost all categories, including cars and televisions. Also, we Indians are tired of having to live with a single product for as many years as we can make it last. Durables in India used to be lifetime purchases. They survived through multiple visits to the service centers, as long as the spare parts were available to keep them going. India now seems to be making up for all those years. Moving up the technology ladder is closely linked with moving up the social ladder. Products today become socially *passé* long before they become technologically obsolete.

Enabling the New

Another key reason that India values technology is its ability to make the old meaningful in a new way. The system of arranged marriages in India has always been about matchmaking. It meant connecting the eligible brides and grooms according to their social status and family background, including caste and region. This system of arranging marriages has now gone online. Online matrimonial services represent one of the most successful adoptions of digital technology by mainstream Indians. In cyber cafés across the country you can find housewives who have sons and daughters of marriageable age, logged on to the matrimonial sites such as shaadi.com and bharatmatrimony.com. Online matrimonial services attained a market size of Rs.140 *crores* ($30 million) in 2007–08, according to the Internet & Mobile Association of India. With a reported growth rate of 40 percent year-on-year, it should reach Rs.750 *crores* ($156 million) by 2012.[1] The category is now coming up with next-level innovations: sites specializing in second marriages (secondshaadi.com) and specific communities, such as those from Gujarat (gujaratimatrimony.com).

The online reservation system of Indian Railways is a prime example of how a population otherwise reluctant to use technology have taken to it for the access that it provides. The website irctc.co.in gets close to 500,000 hits per day. The online reservation service has even fueled peripheral businesses: several cyber cafés in India have made a business of charging a fee to help people book an online railway ticket. The low-cost airline Air Deccan (now Kingfisher Red) took a similar tack when it launched its Rs.1 and Rs.500 airfares, available on a first-come, first-served basis.[2] In 2005, Air Deccan partnered with

Reliance Web World, which already had some 241 broadband centers across 104 cities in India at that time.[3] Mirroring the online railway reservations experience, people queued up in droves at the Reliance Web World centers to book these tickets online.

The college admission process in Maharashtra went online in 2009. Around 200,000 students secured admissions to the first-year junior college (FYJC) through the online mode.[4] Not many of these students had previously known exactly how to use the Internet. Indians feel the incentive to learn new technology when it eases the way to something that was formerly cumbersome or opens new avenues of enjoyment. Mobile phone owners of all types, for instance, have become savvy at downloading and setting up caller ringtones. All these people are not techies who like to experiment with technology for technology's sake; they're simply drawn to the entertainment value of the ringtones.

One of the most successful technology marketing platforms in India was based on health. LG Electronics' televisions came with a feature that automatically adjusted the picture according to the room's ambient light, thereby causing less eyestrain. LG branded this technology Goldeneye and sold the televisions on the platform of "strain free viewing." The advertising for the brand showed a kid watching television in shop fronts because his mother, worried about the strain on his eyes, would not allow him to watch TV at home. Goldeneye came to the rescue of the troubled mother. Regardless of the quality of the storyline, this melodrama around health not only built Goldeneye as a significant brand but also put LG on top of the color television market. LG continued to sell its entire product range of refrigerators, air conditioners, and microwaves on the health platform for many years.

In short, India buys into technology through all sorts of surrogates and meaning systems but very rarely for the technology itself. Marketing the graphic vision of digital technology, rich with high-tech imagery of circuits and chips and gizmos, will likely not be as effective with Indian consumers as it is in the West. To capture the imagination of Indian consumers, technology must be presented as it will be used, interwoven with everyday life, as an enabler of new things and new ways of doing old things.

Vehicles of Social Significance

Transportation in India remains very hierarchical, as a category. The way you commute both reflects and defines who you are. Public transportation, with its close contact and mingling of sweat and body odor, occupies the lowest rung. The intermittent, unpredictable availability of public transportation in India also leaves passengers with little control over their own time. For women there is the threat of sexual advances and harassment in crowded buses or empty bus stops. In this context, personal transportation is a tremendous upgrade, as it liberates you from sharing your space with everyone else and puts you in control of your time. In the 70s and 80s a two-wheeler, like a scooter, was a status symbol in India. Bajaj was the only manufacturer of two-wheelers; there was a long waiting period for their scooters, and customers had no color choice. Despite these hassles, owning a two-wheeler was a big sign of upward mobility, as it gave you your own private transportation space away from the hordes.

As we moved into the twenty-first century, the scooter assumed a more humble role, and cars of various models and sizes became the status symbols. The two-wheeler, however, has sparked another liberation, this time as a scooterette. The scooterette is playing a big role in liberating young women from dependence on public transportation or family members willing to grant them a favor, especially in the smaller towns. Scooty, the scooterette brand of the TVS motor company, has become the generic name for the category. Just like other products of technology, personal mobility in India has social significance beyond its mere functionality. The role of the scooter in gaining personal escape from the public crush and of the Scooty in giving wings to young women will always be larger than their practical role in getting from A to B.

The rules of the road in India are all about encroachment. The more of this public space you can appropriate for yourself, the higher your rank in hierarchy. SUVs in India are not about going off the road; they are about capturing more of the road. The SUVs and their lesser cousins—like the Scorpio from Mahindras or the Safari from Tata—are sold more for their size and attitude than their performance as all-terrain vehicles. A sticker on the rear screen of a Scorpio in Delhi proclaims it: "*Haan sadak mere baap ka hai*" ("Yes, the road belongs to my dad"). These vehicles thus are more about signaling that you are *somebody* on the roads that really belong to *nobody*.

If you observe carefully, you will notice that most of the SUVs and the MUVs on Indian roads have special registration numbers—single digit, or with a pattern like 1 or 1111 or 8888. These are either issued to VIPs or bought for an extra fee by those who want to signal their different (and thereby elevated) status. With dark tinted windows and a special registration number, these vehicles appear to be VIP vehicles, thereby getting special treatment on the road from fellow commuters and sometimes even the traffic police. In an increasingly anonymous world, the SUVs grab attention—"Look at me! I am important!" Is it mere coincidence, then, that these vehicles have become a favorite with the political class as well as the Bollywood celebrities?

Early Upgrades

The car—specifically, its length and its latest-model status—is an extremely sensitive barometer of the owner's position and standing in the society. Its social ranking correlates exactly with its segment in the car category. Tata Motors, having correctly deduced this motivation, launched an entry-level sedan called Indigo CS. The car is cleverly designed so that it falls within the sub-four-meter length bracket, thereby qualifying for all the tax benefits of a small car. However, the length of 3.988 meters allows it to have a very important prestige accoutrement—a trunk. Indigo CS thus is a long-*looking* car with the price advantage of a small car. Its advertising tagline, "The Class Starts Early," captures precisely the motivation of much of India to get to the next level, now. Small-car buyers actually aspire to own a long car; Indigo CS enables an early upgrade.

"Next level now" as a strategy has worked well for car manufactures in India. The game has become a lot more aggressive as almost all of them focus on delivering class-defying features. Maruti Suzuki launched its small car, A Star, at the top end of the entry-level A segment with airbags and antilock braking system (ABS), features that previously had been the prerogative of the sedans.

Similarly, Fiat launched its sedan Linea with rear air conditioning and a host of other features like Blue & Me, which allows voice interface for the onboard music system and the mobile phone. Linea is a C-segment car in pricing, with top-of-the-line D-segment features. Offering the experience of a higher segment for a small premium has been a successful strategy in the Indian car market.

Incentivizing consumers to upgrade is a strategy that consumer durable brands also have played successfully in India. LG Electronics, one of the largest players in the category, has constantly opened up newer segments and upgraded the consumer to the next level of technology. The company, which attained sales of Rs.13,000 *crores* ($2.78 billion) in 2009, aimed to grow by 40 percent to reach Rs.19,000 *crores* ($4.06 billion) in 2010.[5] In the television segment, LG started with the strategy of converting owners of black-and-white television to color TVs and later made the case for flat-screen televisions. The brand is playing the same game in the refrigerator segment, where currently there is a 70:30 split between direct cool refrigerators, an older technology, and frost-free refrigerators, the technology of the future. There is still a high demand for direct cool refrigerators especially from Tier 2 and Tier 3 towns, which are also somewhat recession-proof. Playing the direct cool segment would logically be safer at this point, and brands like Godrej appliances are depending heavily on their direct cool product line. LG, however continues to focus on frost-free models, which are in higher demand in urban areas. They have introduced a new lineup of 27 new models and expect to grow the segment by about 50 percent, realizing sales of over Rs.3,000 *crores* ($642 million) in 2010.[6]

LG's confidence in playing the next-level game in technology is based on its past success in the Indian market. In fact, the consumer durables market in India has always rewarded the first mover—take, for example, the LCD television segment. Samsung has played the flat panel game more aggressively than anybody else, including LG. As a result, while LG won the color television segment, Samsung emerged as the leader in the LCD television segment, with a share of 40 percent. Samsung is now opening up the LED TV segment. The company gave an international launch to three new LED TV models for the Indian market in 2009 and expected about 10 percent of their flat panel sales to come from LED TVs by the end of 2009.[7]

Techno Sheen

Technology in India needs to do more than just appeal to our everyday motivations and practical needs; it also must look sharp and glossy. In the mobile services category, for instance, the two most preferred brands, Vodafone and Airtel, have successfully pulled off this mix of motivation and gloss. Vodafone, which has retained the spirit of its erstwhile brand—Hutch—continues to appeal through its original positioning of childlike simplicity. At the same time, through its premium advertising language and a series of associations, it has also managed to create a sense of a brand that's very international in its appeal. Vodafone's exclusive tie-ins with high-end technology phones such as BlackBerry Storm and Apple iPhone have given it a technological edge, and its associations with lifestyle events such as marathons and theatre festivals have given the brand a certain lifestyle gloss.

Airtel, the more successful of the two brands in its share of the market, connects at a more traditional Indian level of emotion. Its storylines range from celebrating the playful relationship of an on-screen celebrity couple to the bond between father and son. The Airtel brand speaks to a softer emotion in its advertising, with its current message about "*atoot bandhan*" ("unbreakable bonds"). Though some of its latest advertising is trying hard to woo the younger consumer. Airtel has managed to drive its technological gloss by being the first to introduce services such as BlackBerry and by making a big deal about its broadband and mobile bill payment services. Consumers are impressed by the high technology, and at the same time, feel a strong emotional connection with the brand.

The need to be high on tech as well as on the human connection is highlighted by the history of the consumer durable category in India. LG, which drew consumers to its brand through the softer motivation of health, did extremely well in the mainstream segments. Based on its mass premium appeal and aggressive pricing strategy it became the largest home durables brand in the country. But as LG became more closely associated with mainstream success and softer motivations, it lost its tech appeal. Samsung, on the other hand, kept trying to establish a deep emotional connection with the Indian consumer; though it never quite managed this, Samsung did manage to keep its positioning relatively premium and high-tech. With an aggressive line-up of top-end products, Samsung has performed extremely well in the higher-end categories such as LCD TVs. LG, for the lack of that premium and tech appeal, lost out to Samsung in these segments.

Another category that has benefited from playing up a techno sheen is that of two-wheelers. This category was once highly emotion driven. Bajaj Caliber, which carried a tagline "The unshakeable," portrayed a man who doesn't get bowed down by circumstances. The most popular ad of the series was the story of a young man searching for the house of his lost girlfriend; he finally finds her, only to realize that she's now married and has a kid. The unshakeable obviously moves on, taking it all in his stride. Those were the days when even a bike ad left a lump in your throat; today's bike ads put you on the edge of your seat. Bike advertising in India now is totally the domain of stunt masters. From action direction reminiscent of *Kill Bill 2* to the Bollywood stuntmen, bike advertising in India these days is a feat of extreme adventure and high technology. The jury is still out on whether this marketing has gone too far in that direction. One could make a case for returning to deeper motivations, but the gloss of technology and adventure has certainly made the category look more compelling.

The desirability of a technology product is largely embedded in its design, so makers need to focus on product design to create much of the necessary techno sheen allure. Brands like Maruti and Tata have woken up to this. Tata's focus on design in their cars is evident from the Nano—as is the superior styling of the Indigo Manza, the latest version of their flagship car brand Indigo. Maruti's newer models too have a very strong emphasis on design, as evidenced by this press release on the launch of its model Estilo: "The Estilo represents Maruti Suzuki matching pace with the changing taste and lifestyle of vibrant India. The bolder new Estilo is a heady mix of sculpted features, bold designs, new exciting colors."[8] The Indian consumer is asking for brands that connect and products that beckon. Marketers who get this equation right will hit the sweet spot.

Marking a Discontinuity

Technology in India is one area in which the consumer has been less moved by history and heritage. In fact, the verdict has come down rather hard against continuity. Brands such as HMT watches and EC TV (a product of Electronics Corporation of India Limited), trusted names during the 1980s, are off the consumer radar now. The inability of these brands to wipe their slate clean and innovate, led to their sad decline. The trust and heritage that they carried was of little avail compared with other brands that changed with the times and remain a substantial play today.

The difference between those who made it and those who didn't is innovation and reinvention. Bajaj, which was known for its scooter offering in the Indian market, is one such case of a complete makeover from a scooter to a bike brand. Bajaj as a brand had become synonymous with the Indian middle-class ethos. Its advertising slogan, "*Hamaara Bajaj*" ("Our own Bajaj") and lines like "*Chunnu, Munnu de Papa di gaddi*" ("Chunnu, Munnu and their Papa's vehicle") further underscored its middle-class connection. However, when the market began shifting to more youthful and in some way aspirational bikes, Bajaj didn't seem like the brand that you'd want to buy a cool technology bike from. It didn't help much that Hero Honda had the first-mover advantage in 100 cc bikes. Its model CD 100 delivered brilliantly on the proposition of fuel economy with the catchphrase "Fill it, shut it, forget it."

Bajaj launched its first bike, Kawasaki Bajaj 4S Champion, in 1991, about six years after Hero Honda's debut. But Bajaj had yet to establish the brand image of a bike company, never mind the myriad of Bajaj scooters that inhabited the Indian roads and many more Bajaj scooter moments in people's memories. Bajaj also ran a remixed version of the *Hamaara Bajaj* ad with shots of "tradition meets modernity" and the claim "We are changing." While all these efforts together signaled an intention to change, they were at best a halfway attempt, as Bajaj was trying to somehow mix the old with the new. The remixed version of its old advertisement epitomized this reluctance to break with the past and a desire to change—but with continuity.

What had been Bajaj's asset to that point—its equity with the Indian middle class in the scooters category—could have become its liability, but for its launch of Pulsar in 2001. Bajaj Pulsar, as an idea, retained nothing of the Bajaj that people knew. It presented a completely new, discontinuous face of Bajaj and its bikes. In its styling Pulsar had an aggressive and mean look—a rather full-grown masculine design. This was a clear movement away from the kind of bikes Bajaj had launched in its prior search for a new path, caught somewhere between the rounded scooters and the macho bike look. The Pulsar advertising, too, was a marked departure from the communication—loaded with traditional Indian coding—that had previously come from the Bajaj stable. The Pulsar ad, which signed off as "Definitely Male," showed two nurses in a maternity ward unveiling the bike and crying out loud, "It's a boy!" Slightly scandalous coming from the house of Bajaj, this created the precise dissonance that the brand needed to shake off its conservative past. Pulsar—the whole package—marked a sharp discontinuity in the brand Bajaj and paved the way for a successful run in the bike category.

What Pulsar did for Bajaj, Scorpio did for Mahindra & Mahindra. Mahindras were known in India as manufacturers of the Mahindra Jeep at one end and tractors at the other. After a lukewarm response to its MUV Voyager, Mahindras launched its game-changing vehicle Scorpio. What worked for Scorpio was the fact that in its styling, performance, and positioning it was a complete departure from the Mahindra & Mahindra that people had known to that point. The vehicle, positioned as a car plus, not only upgraded the C segment car buyers to an MUV but also ended up expanding the then nascent utility vehicle market. The company now seems to be viewed as a credible player in the utility vehicle segment: its latest offering in the segment, Xylo, has also found a fair amount of favor with the Indian consumer.

It's apparent that in order to regain consumer preference in the technology segment, brands with a history need to completely let go of it. They need to embrace a fresh new approach, not only in their offerings but also in their thinking. Many trusted brands that refuse to cut the umbilical cord with the past have struggled to find favor with consumers. A discontinuous offering like the Nano not only ensures its own success but also galvanizes the parent brand, in this case the Tata Group. But at the same time an offering like the Indicom, Tata's mobile service venture, has neither added much to the parent brand nor been able to find real success. Tata Indicom has been held back by the dynamics of the CDMA category, which suffers from a lack of choice in premium handsets and mass-market image. Tata Indicom hasn't achieved the break with the past that a technology brand needs, especially as it's a Tata offering still somewhat tied to its historical image.

The corollary is that brands like Airtel—homegrown upstarts—have done well, despite having no heritage or tradition of trust. Similarly, Korean brands such as Hyundai, LG, and Samsung, which started with a zero equity with Indian consumer, have captured a more than fair share of the market because they captured people's imaginations with fresh product offerings. In contrast, foreign brands with significant brand equity even before they entered India—such as Sony, Ford, and Mitsubishi—have not been able to generate a surprising performance in India because they failed to surprise India with their offerings. When it comes to the technology space, Indian consumers seem to be unimpressed by history and continuity. Every brand, it seems, starts at ground zero with them. There are no bonus points for having a heritage, and there's no disadvantage to being a new kid on the block.

High Tech, High Connection

Unlike money, beauty, entertainment, and personal care, technology in India is a new game. There are no cultural codes or social mores to guide or govern the consumption of technology. Yet in India, marketers need to interpret technology in culturally familiar terms. India buys into technology through all sorts of surrogates such as health, opportunity access, a sense of upgrading, and so on. In many ways, technology with all its offerings and opportunities is a bridge from where Indians have been to where they want to go.

Technology, being an outside influence, offers the allure of the unknown. It's something that needs to be acquired, as there are no prior generations of technology traditions. This makes high-tech products objects of desire. Marketers can heighten that appeal with a glossy design, present the benefits in familiar terms, and play up the potential for upward mobility. But in a labor-abundant country, the promise of convenience or efficiency has limited appeal.

Building a technology brand in India is thus both easy and tough. It's easy because you don't need established brand equity to be able to excite consumers and their imagination. It's tough because technology brands need to deliver on many levels, even seemingly opposite ones such as emotional appeal and tech gloss. Technology brands can actually learn from the structure of Bollywood cinema, which is adept at existing on multiple planes simultaneously. A movie like *Om Shanti Om*, for instance, has a seriously melodramatic storyline, typical of Indian cinema. But it renders this with all the gloss that India today wants to see, from bronzed bodies with six-pack abs to dazzling dance sequences and designer costumes.

It's important in the Indian marketplace for a winning technology brand to take a leadership stance. The Indian consumer has always rewarded a well-executed first move. LG became the biggest consumer durable brand by steadily upgrading the consumer to the next level of technology. Samsung won the premium LCD TV game with the same strategy. And Hero Honda found its footing by launching an economical motorcycle way back in 1985, upgrading the Indian middle class from scooters to motorcycles. The consumer who has no sociocultural benchmarks for judging this category and wants to make sure that he stays ahead of the curve is drawn by the "latest" that's available.

Technology has visibly transformed many lives at the personal level by making India the world's biggest back office and generating jobs for millions while helping another few find their life partners. However, the power of technology in India lies not so much in its ability to make our lives more convenient and efficient but in the enhanced self-image it offers us. We feel a sense of growth and new possibilities with every technological product we buy—and that is fertile ground for marketers.

6

BRANDING THE BAZAAR

THE LOGIC OF INDIAN BRANDS
AND RETAILING

The Effect, Not the Cause

Much has been said about the boom in the retailing industry in India. The resulting euphoria, which led to a mindless land-grab strategy by most players, caused an equal degree of recoil when the world economic slowdown began. The truth is that retailing is essentially the face of consumer demand being generated at the back end, and its sales graphs are bound to fluctuate along with changes in consumer sentiment. At the same time, a country with a GDP growth rate of 8.5 percent (2010–11) and a mindset opening up to new experiences is bound to flock to the shop windows filled with consumer goods that beckon them. The fact that retailing in India is a high-potential sector poised for tremendous transformation is an *effect* of the recent unleashing of consumption desires, not a *cause*. Retailing is, after all, just the marketplace where consumers interface with what they will consume. A population whose values, attitudes, and behavior are being swept by winds of change will certainly demand that the marketplace change to keep up with those changes.

In the past decade or so, the façade of the Indian consumer market has undergone a complete makeover, all in the customer's favor. Bank account holders who once stood in long queues in dusty public sector banks now walk into an air-conditioned kiosk, punch a few ATM keys, and take the cash. Customers once dependent on the whims of the shopkeeper's teenage help if they wanted to check out a new fairness cream are now wooed to sample it at promotion desks; shoppers who had to buy clothes without being able to try them on now try as many as they want without the fear of being sneered at by the shop owner. This has happened across various sectors in retail, starting with banking and expanding to apparel, to packaged foods, and now to fresh fruits and vegetables.

Most of the efforts in this round of the retail revolution, how-ever, have gone into building an experience where none previously existed. This round has therefore been about establishing the first level of organized retailing. Whether it's a hypermarket or a food court or a multiplex, each of the respective categories has ushered in the next level of experience for the Indian consumer. But even in this foundational phase of category building, there have been clear hits and misses. What clearly hasn't worked: a direct bor-rowing of international formats without incorporating any local understanding, or a blind adherence to the operational rules of a retail format. What has worked, and separated the winners from the losers: an astute understanding of the needs and behavior of the Indian consumer.

The Future Group, whose Big Bazaar venture is one of the most celebrated case studies of Indian retailing, has achieved this by keeping a sensitive finger on the pulse of the Indian consumer. The hypermarket chain, positioned as *"Is se sasta aur achcha kahin nahin* ("Nowhere is it cheaper or better"), taps into the value-conscious mindset of Indians. The entire store has been designed to give Indian shoppers an experience similar to that of a bazaar—the traditional conglomeration of shops full of hustle, bustle, and chaos. The strategy of "organized chaos," as the owners of the retail chain characterize it, has brought Indians to Big Bazaar outlets in droves, even as their competitors—which followed the international formats of clean and efficient stores—longed for half as many footfalls.

The Big Bazaar experience has proven that retailing in India is not about formats and templates; rather, it's about understanding the consumers' needs and meeting them with an experience that they will enjoy. Shopping is the chief form of entertainment for the Indian middle-class consumer. It is a full-blown event, part of a larger ritual of the family outing. Whereas in the past it would be built around the bazaar (a congregation of shops), today it's built around the malls, with Big Bazaar and McDonald's as part of the circuit. In Ahmedabad, for instance, a Big Bazaar outlet, the Iskcon temple, and a McDonald's restaurant are located in an almost perfect triangle, which has become a popular circuit for families. An outing to this place makes for a perfect package: a small dose of spirituality, some shopping, and some eating out. Understanding such nuances of behavior and ways of life is essential for success with the Indian consumer.

To better understand retailing, we need to better understand the drivers of consumer demand. Changes in several factors—demographic patterns, affluence levels, and consumer mind-sets—are giving rise to new dynamics in the Indian consumer market. Understanding these idiosyncrasies of the Indian market can be valuable for tapping into new potential.

The Changing Shape of the Indian Market

The shape of the Indian consumer market is changing, owing to a change in the shape of the population and income levels. In terms of both population and the size of aggregate consumption, India has been a pyramid-shaped market with a broad bottom level. Most of the active consuming class was in this mass segment of the market. As shown in Figure 6.1, the segments are progressively narrower, with a small middle segment and a very small premium segment.

But with rising incomes and changing population demographics, what was once the lowest segment of the market is becoming the middle segment as consumers move up. Earlier, the larger Indian middle class could afford a two-wheeler scooter at best, in time upgraded to a small car like Maruti 800, and made do with a desert cooler in the living room. The middle-class Indian today can afford a B-segment car like the Hyundai Santro and has air-conditioning in the bedroom and a frost-free refrigerator in the kitchen. In a

Figure 6.1. The Changing Shape of India's Population, Income, and Consumption Profile.

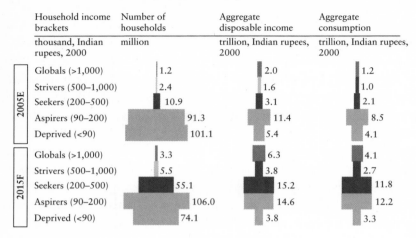

Source: *McKinsey Global Institute.*

NCAER – Future Capital Research study that lists 20 cities to watch, across the 20 cities, 70 percent of car owners are middle class. And the middle class makes up more than 60 percent of owners in the computer, AC, washing machine, and microwave oven categories.[1] The middle segment of the market in India is swelling, with an overall upgrading in the lives of Indian consumers, in part because of an overall increase in income and also because products and services formerly inaccessible at certain price points have now become accessible.

Today it's possible, for instance, to buy a car like the Tata Nano for $2,000. As the speed of technological obsolescence increases and the manufacturers' interest in upgrading consumers to the next level grows, manufacturers have lowered the prices of old technology products in favor of the new. For example, manufacturers wanting to upgrade the air conditioner market to split ACs have allowed a drop in the price of window air conditioners. The same thing has happened with color televisions in the light of LCDs and with personal care products such as Lux soap in the light of the more premium Lux International. What was previously at the premium end across categories has now reached down to the middle of the market, while the consumer who was part of the entry-level masses has upgraded with a new ability to afford the premium. Led by the upgrading trend among consumers and the affordability trend in brands and products, the middle of the Indian market is swelling, transforming the pyramid to a more pot-bellied shape, as shown in Figure 6.2.

There are changes at the top end of the market as well. With the top-income segment of the population getting richer, what was once premium for them isn't so premium anymore. The mainstream segment has swelled, with the middle-class consumers able to afford what was once beyond their reach. This change has two implications. First, many products and services that were once part of the premium segment are now part of the mainstream. Second, a whole new premium segment is emerging, with new products and services catering to the newly affluent Indian consumer. This is the new market for luxury in India. In housing, for instance, this segment has seen several launches by builders such as Lodhas and India Bulls in Mumbai and DLF and Unitech in Delhi. Brands such as Audi and BMW in luxury sedans, Jean Claude Beguine in spa salons, and

Figure 6.2. The Changing Shape of the Indian Market—From Pyramid to Potbellied.

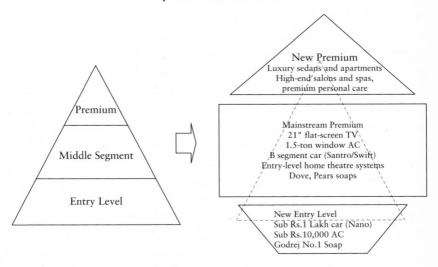

Not to scale; for representation purposes only.

Neutrogena and L'Oreal in personal care are serving this market. This top end of the market always existed in India, but until recently its numbers were too small to make a business case for any luxury brand to launch here. Most of these people thus shopped abroad and yearned for these experiences back home. With rising affluence levels, however, marketing to the super-premium end of the market in India today is making business sense.

In the downturn year 2008–09, even as the mass market was a bit slow, the premium segment presented a strong opportunity. On the retail front, two big luxury destinations have sprung up: the UB City mall, spread across 125,000 square feet in Bangalore, and the DLF Emporio mall, with 320,000 square feet in Delhi. In luxury sedans, Audi exceeded its annual sales of 2008 in the first eight months of 2009, reporting growth of 62 percent compared to the same period in 2008. According to an Ernst & Young study, the Indian wellness market which stands at Rs.11,000 *crores* ($2.27 billion) is set to grow at a compounded annual growth rate of 30 to 35 percent for the next five years.[2] Players in the wellness space are now planning for expansion; Evolve Medspa, which opened its first center in Mumbai in April 2008, now aims to expand its presence to 45 centers across 12 cities in India by 2012.

The other big change in the market structure is that the cut-off point of what is considered the consuming class is shifting downward. What has been projected as the fortune at the bottom of the pyramid is now becoming a reality, adding a new entry-level segment to the Indian consumer market.[3] This is the segment that needs players to innovate and find new business models. Everybody—from the modern retailers like the Future Group to the mobile phone players like Nokia—is charting a strategy for this consumer. This is the market, for instance, for mobile phones at a weekly installment of $2 per week—an initiative being launched by Nokia in India. The new entry level is also the market for fast-moving consumer goods (FMCG) in lower SKUs, white goods such as semi-automatic washing machines, and products across categories that allow these consumers membership in the world of consumption. (See Figure 6.2.)

Within these segments, however, there is clearly a wide range of play. The mainstream segment itself ranges from mass premium at

Figure 6.3. A Wide Range of Play Within Segments.

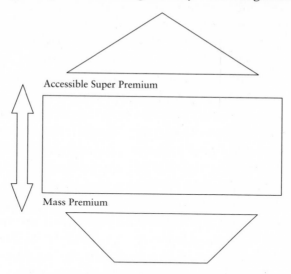

Accessible Super Premium

Mass Premium

Not to scale; for representation purposes only.

the bottom to accessible super-premium at the top. (See Figure 6.3.) This is a segment that starts with brands such as Godrej No. 1 soaps and Clinic Plus shampoos and goes up to brands such as Garnier, Nivea, Lakme, and the Vivel Di Wills range launched by ITC. In readymade shirts, for instance, the segment starts at Rs.699 with brands such as John Players and goes up to Rs.1,599 with brands such as Arrow. In cars, it can start with a compact car such as the Maruti Swift and reach all the way up to a sedan such as the SX4. Similarly, the entry level typically starts with a two-wheeler from Bajaj or TVS or Hero Honda and can go all the way up to a Tata Nano or a Maruti 800. In FMCG, it can start with the sachets and smaller SKUs of various brands, such as Chik shampoo at 50 paisa, and go up to brands such as Pond's and even Fair & Lovely.

Credible Stretch

Many brands and businesses in India have struggled with a key question: can a mass brand ever upgrade to the next level? And a related question: can extending a premium brand down to lower segments erode its carefully established image? Specific answers can be found only through close scrutiny of the brand's core and the category's context. However, there seems to be an inherent logic in the market that suggests there is a credible range for such a stretch (see Figure 6.4). A brand like Big Bazaar, the largest hypermarket chain in the country, stretches across the mainstream segment, drawing the shopper for an Rs.250 ($5) shirt as well as a housewife looking for expensive Barilla pasta. Their cosmetic counters offer Olay Total effects at one end and Pond's moisturizing lotion at the other. The brand Big Bazaar has managed to straddle the entire mainstream segment from mass premium to accessible super-premium with ease.

There are many other examples of brands straddling the mainstream segment with relative ease. LG, as an electronics brand, has managed to be as relevant to the buyer of a 21-inch flat-screen TV as to the buyer of a front-loading washing machine. Maruti Suzuki started out selling the Maruti 800, a small car

Figure 6.4. The Range of Credible Stretch.

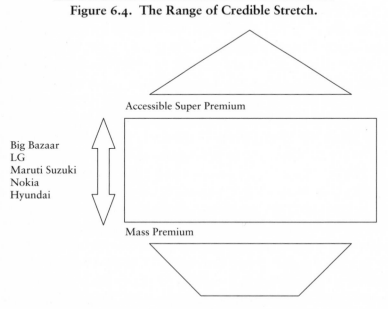

Not to scale; for representation purposes only.

in the A segment, and has successfully established its presence in the B as well as the C segment with its models Swift and SX4, respectively. Similarly, Hyundai has had a good run in the B segment with its flagship model, the Santro, as well as in the C segment with the Accent. Nokia too has done well with its models from entry level right up to the N97. It's apparent that brands have successfully managed to straddle the range from mass premium to accessible super-premium in India. Between these two points in the Indian market lies the range of credible stretch, where a single brand can successfully play with offerings at multiple price points.

The elasticity of the credible range, however, gives way when a brand tries to cross over to the next segment. Mainstream brands trying to upgrade to the super-premium segment or entry-level brands attempting upgrade to the mainstream segment have found it difficult to do so. For example, despite all its success in the mainstream car market, Hyundai as a brand in India has not been able to crack the D segment. Sonata, Hyundai's offering in the premium D segment has failed to take off even after several re-launch attempts. Similarly, LG, which has managed to capture a significant market share in the mainstream segment, has not been able to replicate that success in premium categories such as LCD televisions, where Samsung has stolen the march. Though the Big Bazaar model has succeeded with middle class consumers, it's questionable whether it can stretch the current format to include the next-level consumers. Nirma—which made its success as an entry-level detergent, giving Unilever's Surf a run for its money—has also found it difficult to break into the next segment under the same brand.

Indian consumers are hungry to upgrade. And when they escape from their current level to the next, they obviously want to acquire new symbols worthy of their new status. Moving on to the next level sometimes means leaving their old one behind. Therefore their brands and their meaning system also must change. Over time, brands get pigeonholed in this hierarchy of upgrading. The hierarchy, though, is flexible within a certain range. Brands are therefore able to credibly stretch to cover a range within the same level, but a change to a new level calls for a change in signifiers and often a different set of brands.

Access Brands

There are two undeniable realities of the Indian consumer market today: one is its size, which, even after dividing into segments discussed in this chapter, promises significant potential. The second is the constant need for upgrading across these segments. The two realities together have created a market with tremendous momentum. The millions of people transitioning between the segments make India a market that is constantly churning. This means that at any given time there is a huge, untapped consumer demand on the borderlines between the segments. It seems there are faultlines between the segments, awaiting products and services with the right price-value equation, which can tip consumers from one segment to the next.

Nirma is a well-known case of building a mass detergent brand in India. Nirma's success came from capitalizing on a similar potential in the detergent market: the borderline between the locally made washing soaps and Hindustan Lever's Surf. Nirma offered a washing powder that was superior to the washing soaps that a large section of Indian consumers were using yet lower in quality than Surf, which most of India couldn't afford at that time. Karsanbhai Patel—the man behind the idea—bridged the gap by selling Nirma for Rs.3.50 a kilogram, compared with the Surf price of Rs.15. At that time, when the annual quantity of high-end detergents sold in India was 25,000 tons, Nirma created a new category between the low-quality soaps and high-quality Surf. Nirma built a market of 300,000 tons by supplying the consumer who wanted to upgrade from the lower segment but could not afford the next-level product.

Nirma detergent is what we term an *access brand*. Access brands make their category accessible to the consumer segment below. They tap into categories of products that are out of reach for some consumers and make them reachable. Access brands often redefine value in that particular category, just as Nirma did in detergents. Clearly, the price-value equation is a critical component of the access brand strategy. But it's important not to view these brands as mere rip-offs of their premium counterparts. It's true that most of these brands emulate the imagery created by the category leader and are parasitic in that sense. But successful access brands command their own trust within their consumer segments and stand for value and consistent delivery—the most basic tenets of building successful brands.

There are several instances of local players successfully finding niches for such brands across categories. Action, a maker of affordable sports shoes based in Delhi, created an access brand to the category created by Nike. Action shoes let the segment of consumers who cannot afford Nike partake of the experience created by the premium sports brand. Another example is Kakaji Namkeens, a local producer of snacks and sweets based in Chaman Ganj in New Delhi. For the same price—say, Rs.10—charged by its multinational corporation (MNC) counterparts like Frito-Lay, Kakaji Namkeens always packs in at least 50 grams more of its product. Similarly, Parle—an established player in biscuits, confectioneries, and snacks—launched its Musst chips (wafers) with a promise of 50 percent more than its competitive brands. In its advertising Parle claims to have put the money they would have spent on hiring expensive models into giving extra value to its customers. Brands such as Kakaji Namkeens, Action, and Parle's Musst are positioned exactly at the cusp between a generic commodity and a brand. They carry enough assurance of quality and quantity to consistently meet consumer expectations. At the same time, they spend very little on advertising and promotion to build any image. They instead take advantage of the image created by the leading brand in the category.

Jyothy Laboratories came into the limelight with their Ujala brand of fabric whitener, a liquid concentrate that delivered an upgraded experience over the incumbent Robin Blue, a powder whitener brand from Reckitt Benckiser. Ujala made it possible for the economy consumer to wear white shirts as immaculate as those of the richer class. The brand in many ways broke through the class divide—as Robin Blue, because of its pricing, had been a prerogative of the upper middle class. Ujala was not only a more modern offering because of its liquid formula but also more affordable. Jyothy Laboratories has followed up this success with its offering in the mosquito repellant category. Its Maxo brand—which competes against Reckitt's Mortein products and Goodknight products from Godrej Sara Lee, among others—follows the same formula of innovation and value as Ujala. Jyothy Laboratories have thus created an entire business of access brands. In their own words, the company's founding ideals are "untapped markets, innovative products that cater to the common man . . . Jyothy Laboratories through its market analysis looks out for a vacuum that can be filled."[4]

Priya Gold is another brand that has entered a category—in this case, biscuits—dominated by established players (Parle and Britannia) and captured a significant share of the market. Priya Gold brought access to the relatively premium world of cream, butter, and chocolate biscuits to consumers at reasonable prices. Its advertising, with the tagline "*Haq se maango*" ("Demand it rightfully"), exhorted consumers to ask for Priya Gold, because everybody has the right to good health and taste. Surya Food and Agro, owner of the brand, has reached sales of Rs.400 *crores* ($82.4 million) and, riding its success in biscuits, has also ventured into the categories of juices, chocolates, and confectioneries.

The consumer desire for upgrading and the ensuing opportunities for companies to create new markets between segments has also led to a lot of play in the car industry. Most of the new-launch energies in the Indian car market today are focused on these borderlines between segments. With almost every new car launch, the definition of value in each of the segments is redefined. Ford, by pricing its C segment model Ikon at the B-plus segment price, made a success of an otherwise sluggish launch. Similarly, the Tata Indica was launched on the promise of "more car per car," thereby opening up new value in the B segment. The borderline between B and C, for instance, has seen significant activity. Honda launched its compact car Jazz at the premium end of the hatchback segment, with pricing close to its sedan Honda City. Hyundai placed its i20 model in this same borderline zone. Clearly there are consumers waiting to be upgraded by brands that can fill the gaps.

Access brands thus may not be confined to the lower segments of the market. They can happen anywhere in the market where there is a gap between two segments and there is a consumer base ready to be upgraded. A brand such as Peter England in men's apparel is an access brand for the mainstream segment, with shirts starting at Rs.595. At the same time, brands like Koutons and Turtle are access brands to the premium segment, with their shirts starting at Rs.799. The idea is to redefine the value points to make the segment accessible to people who didn't have access to it before. Although value is almost always a critical part of access brands, it's more than just selling things cheap. It's about placing the same quality and the experience—and, more often than not, a product that's considered premium—within consumers' reach.

The Indigenous Instinct

It's likely more than just a coincidence that most who success-fully tap such opportunities are local entrepreneurs rather than business-educated multinationals. Whether it's Karsanbhai Patel, who created Nirma; Kishore Biyani, who has built the largest retailing company in India, Future Group; or C. K. Ranganathan, whose CavinKare made shampoos accessible with 50-paisa sachets, there is something about their sense of the opportunity and the pulse of the consumer that no market research or new product development funnel has been able to better.

One of the biggest advantages of these entrepreneurs is being able to keep an ear to the ground. Paras Pharma, an entrepre-neurial company based in Ahmedabad, has sales of more than Rs.400 *crores* ($82 million). The company seems to specialize in spotting specific consumer issues and creating categories around them. For instance, cracked heels were never seen as a prob-lem in India; they were a reality that women lived with. Paras Pharma spotted this as an opportunity and created a new cat-egory with their Krack cream. Thanks to consistent advertising, having cracked heels has now become a matter of social embar-rassment—and selling a solution became a whole new profit cen-ter for Paras Pharma.

In a similar way, the company latched onto the fact that in a hot and humid climate like India's, itching was a common problem. The existing solution, B Tex ointment, was seen as old and fuddy-duddy and had done little to establish a category. Paras launched Itch Guard, a brand named around the problem that it solved. With advertising support as good as any FMCG brand, Itch Guard single-handedly created this category and made the act of public scratching a public embarrassment. Paras Pharma's success in zeroing in on insights extremely specific to Indian consumers and converting them into profitable brands speaks to the power of indigenous instinct.

Another example of such astute local thinking is Anchor's launch of vegetarian toothpaste. Vegetarians in India are many, and ensuring that they are not violating this edict of their religion is a big preoccupation for them. Anchor, an extremely successful brand in electric switches, ventured into the FMCG market with the launch of Anchor White toothpaste in 1997. The brand was positioned as India's first British Dental Health Society–certified 100 percent vegetarian toothpaste. Anchor also realized the power of retail support in an established category like oral care. Competitive pricing and high trade margins worked to tilt the playing field in its favor. When, in 2002, this brand of toothpaste from a company better known for electric switches reached the number three position in its category, it was further proof of the power of indigenous insight—and the innovation that flows from it.

Another key trait of an entrepreneurial setup is its fast time to market. While large companies are busy building plans and researching the opportunities, entrepreneurially driven companies are out there cashing in on them. For instance, many local germ-protection products were quick to position themselves against the global swine flu scare of 2009. The opportunity was answered with brands like Sudhol in Maharashtra, which spread awareness through local media like radio. The Aditya Birla group, which had previously launched its facial tissue brand Kara on the skin care platform, was also quick to spot the opportunity, launching a brand of hand-sanitizing tissues called Handy.

A similar fast time to market has been demonstrated by local players in the fashion space. It's important to understand that the mass of Indian consumers get their fashion inspiration from Bollywood. Fashion fads change from one Bollywood hit to another. The key therefore is to match the fashion production cycles to the speed of fads sparked by Bollywood. Generally speaking, the time span from when a fashion fad emerges from Bollywood to when it appears in the shops of Linking Road in Mumbai or Sarojini Nagar in Delhi is no more than a few weeks—a feat not so easy for the larger, more established players to accomplish.

The third key characteristic of indigenous instinct is a certain directness of approach. These brands and companies are free from any kind of encumbrances. Paras Pharma's Set Wet range of deodorants and hair styling is an interesting example. The brand is positioned in the space of irresistible sexuality and sports a tagline "Very Very Sexy." The television spots for Set Wet, shot in international locales with international models, are a radical departure from the conservative image of the company and its established brands. The Set Wet product range and the advertising language would hardly be identified by consumers as a brand from the same people who make Krack cream and Itch Guard. Certainly, the language of the brand is discontinuous from the perceived value system of the company. But it demonstrates the fact that this company is willing to do whatever it takes to win in the category; that its business considerations are in no way encumbered by the value systems of its owners, who belong to a traditional Gujrati family.

Directness is also apparent in the positioning of the Big Bazaar chain: "*Is se sasta aur achcha kahin nahin*" ("Nowhere is it cheaper or better"). The fact that the Indian consumer wanted things cheaper was an understanding that most of the Indian marketers lived with. But until the Future Group took the plunge, nobody had had the gumption to so overtly make this fact their competitive advantage. Big Bazaar, however, has stated it right up front. They have even tapped into the Indian practice of saving scrap—like old newspapers and steel and plastic remnants—with a resale value. Big Bazaar actually celebrates a *bhangaar* festival at which they offer customers shopping money in exchange for their old scrap.

This indigenous ingenuity is creating new value points in the Indian market structure. A keen ear to the ground, an extremely short time to market, and an unabashed ability to be direct and not held back by niceties has helped these local players redefine value and opportunity. Not that such ability and consequent success are the sole prerogative of local players. However, even the outside players who have successfully managed to open new markets in India—such as LG in consumer durables and Hyundai in cars—have done so based on similar entrepreneurial traits. Thus any marketer to the Indian consumer would do well to consider, understand, and possibly adopt these particularly Indian ways of doing business.

Following the Market Logic

The first round of modern retailing in India has been about one size fits all. Most of the efforts and energies have gone into putting the basic infrastructure into place and getting the back end up and running. In this round, therefore, the propositions that have catered to the middle segment have seen success. But as the shape of the Indian market changes and two other critical segments emerge, at the top and the bottom, it makes good business sense for retailing to move beyond the mainstream.

Evidence suggests that the retail landscape is already responding and beginning to mirror the changing shape of the Indian market. At the top end of the market, for instance, jewelry manufacturer and retailer Gitanjali Group is joining forces with MMTC (a public-sector enterprise and India's largest international trading company) to set up a chain of exclusive retail outlets selling hallmarked gold and diamond jewelry. The chain, called Shuddi Sampurna Vishwas, will have around 60 stores across India. Similarly, many other aspects of the premium market, such as health care and health insurance, offer ready potential. Much of the conversation around health care in India has been about its underpenetration and the opportunities at the bottom of the pyramid. With the increasing vulnerability of urban life and an increase in lifestyle diseases, the potential at the top end for health care and insurance providers is booming too. Max Bupa, which launched its health insurance business in India in April 2010, with a paid-up capital of Rs.151 *crores* ($32.5 million) plans to increase it to Rs.700 *crores* ($150.6 million) over a period of five years.[5] Its flagship product, Heartbeat, is available in three different levels of coverage—silver, gold, and platinum—with the platinum level offering a host of exclusive services for the top-segment consumers. Across categories, retailing at the top end of the Indian market is ready to be opened up at high margins.

The dynamics at the bottom end of the market in India is completely different. With high volumes waiting to be converted, this segment will need ground-up innovations in retailing, just as it has in most other categories. Value and access will continue to be the key drivers for this market, and the need for specifically relevant solutions cannot be overemphasized. The model of retailing for this end of the market calls for innovation; a consortium of local players brought together under one roof is one possible beginning. This could be an upgraded or branded version of the current Indian bazaar (traditional open shopping area) where multiple sellers come together in one area to sell their wares. The current bazaar model has no common umbrella that can drive economies of scale and benefits of belonging for the entire consortium. Future Group's KB's Wholesale Markets—which is being designed to act as a rural hub for small manufacturers, traders, and retailers—is one such innovation.

The middle segment of the market will continue to develop new fault lines and opportunities to further upgrade the consumer. There is opportunity for learning in this space from the indigenous instinct with which Indian entrepreneurs have built brands and categories where none existed before. This segment of the market has seen a lot of action recently, and most of the obvious opportunities have already been exploited. This segment thus needs marketers to take a fresh look at consumer needs and habits and respond with offerings and messaging they have not experienced before. Maybe the small-town consumer who has only been to a single screen theater is ready for an upgraded multiplex experience; perhaps the Indian middle class is ready to sample some international street food, if only a retail chain would step in and offer it—the mainstream segment has a big appetite for continuous upgrading and fresh combinations.

Linking the Haves and the Have-Nots

The fast pace of change in last 15 years has created two Indias— one that has benefited from the India growth story and another that hasn't. Retailing as an industry can in some ways help bridge the gap between these two. First and foremost, retail creates a space that is classless and thereby brings various sections of society together under the same roof. In a Big Bazaar outlet, for instance, there is merchandise that caters to consumers across socioeconomic classes. When Gurgaon, the satellite city of Delhi, was being developed, real estate developers bought large plots of land from local farmers and landowners. When the malls and other facilities appeared on these properties, they became like tourist attractions for the former inhabitants. However, many of these local people actually made large sums of money selling off their land and later wanted to upgrade their standard of living. These malls have now turned out to be their shopping spots, as much as they are for the urban migrants to this suburbia.

Benefits for the Backend

The ability of retail shopping spaces to unite people across classes may be limited. But the ability of its back end to bring economic advantages to those who would otherwise remain untouched by the shopping spaces is much higher. That's because a healthy retail industry can only be built on the foundation of a strong supply chain. Retailers are investing in technology and procurement processes, which have led to a better utilization of agricultural resources and better prices for the producer. For instance, the demand created by retailing in Delhi has stimulated cultivation and resulting income of the Rawain valley to the north of Dehradun in Uttarakhand. According to an article by Bart Minten and Ashok Gulati in the *Times of India* (September 2009), due to the newly established local collection centers, the cultivation of off-seasonal vegetables has risen from about 5 percent of the cultivable area to about 50 percent over the last 8 to 10 years. Whereas 10 years ago, some 5 percent of the farmers in the area cultivated seasonal vegetables, now almost all of them do. Reports suggest that about six million farmers would benefit from commerce with top retail companies in India by 2010.[6]

Protecting Mom and Pop

One big concern with corporate retailing the world over has been the future of mom-and-pop establishments—in India, the local *kirana* (grocery) shops. The Indian retailing trajectory up to this point suggests that these are not going away in a hurry. In fact, many of them have actually woken up to the competition and have been transforming both their merchandise and their level of service. The truth is that the benefits of home delivery and the monthly credit line that the neighborhood grocer offers are hard for any chain retailer to beat. Although many Indian consumers, especially in larger cities, are shifting to the hypermarkets for their monthly shopping, for their day-to-day needs, quick refills, and emergency needs, they still depend on the *kirana*.

In more ways than one, retailing as an idea seems to have the potential to make the India growth story more inclusive. Driven by pure economics, the retail space in India is turning out to be more equal than any other. It's helping equalize the old social hierarchy in many ways. It's about upgrading the consumer by building bridges in between the existing segments. It's also about including the newer segments at the bottom end. Meanwhile, the developments at the supply end are making the other India a clear beneficiary of the retail boom. The small entrepreneurial mom-and-pops too are mostly growing along with the retailing boom, rather than being vanquished by it. The bazaar, in its new branded form, seems to hold promise for all. It is rewarding indigenous thinking and encouraging local production at the back end, while its front doors are opening wider, inviting in consumers not included before.

7

YOUTH VERSUS YOUTHFUL

BUILDING YOUTH BRANDS IN
A YOUTHFUL COUNTRY

Squeezed Out

Despite the fact that India has one of the youngest populations in the world—with a median age of 24, and 207 million people in the age range of 15 to 24—there are no mainstream youth brands in India. This may be, in part, because in terms of sheer numbers and purchasing power, the 25- to 44-year-olds—the "youthful"— are a much larger (350 million) and thus more tempting segment. Focusing solely on youth always means sacrificing other segments, and sacrifices in business and marketing are not always easy to make. But more than that, even brands that want to speak effectively to youth often fall into the trap of speaking more to the "youthful" in personality than the "young" in fact. Youthfulness is a characteristic easily acquired, but being truly young entails a motivation that is not so easy to crack.

Most models and frameworks of building youth brands and mapping youth insights have a Western origin. In the Western context, youth is almost always a generation pitted against its elders. Rebellion is the key starting point. Adventure, music, and other symbols of "cool" have formed a perfect recipe for creating cult brands that rebel against the system. This model of tapping youth presupposes a larger microcosm of young versus old, so marketers are continually searching for what's cool among the young. Because the behavioral distance between youth and other age ranges in these societies is significant, it's easy to rally youth around such points of difference.

This model, however, is far less appropriate in an environment like India's, in which nearly everything and everyone is young. India's largest consuming class population of about 50 million (urban, top three socioeconomic classes) is in the age range of 25 to 45 years. But most of them behave more like teenagers who are just turning 19. Why 19? The Indian consumer is precisely 19 years old, as that's how long it has been since Indian markets were liberalized. With a newfound affordability and new avenues of consumption, everybody in India is young. This goes not just for the people but also for the brands. A society held back by scarcity and a self-restrained value system built around it is suddenly opening up to gratifying the pangs of desire. And marketers, in their attempt to be attractive to these consumers with deep pockets, have realized that being "youthful" is an easy way to sell.

But when everybody feels youthful and all brands are youthful, the real casualty is the young. For those in the age range of 15 to 25, the preceding generation is in competition not only for the brands they can wear but also the places they can hang out and the fashionable things they can do. Pepsi in India is fast becoming a family drink, and Levis are as much a brand for the intern as for the CEO. In the common ground of youth as an age and youthful as an attitude, the real youth of India have nothing that they can call exclusively their own. The youth in India are thus squeezed out by the youthful. This leaves Indian youth searching for that which they can truly call their own.

Not a Different Species

The traditional marketing paradigm is designed to look at the consumer from a distance. Consumers are another box in any brand model. Their identified needs fill this box. Consumers are out there to be met and reported about. Research thus is designed to be done from a distance. This frame of reference is even more pronounced in the case of youth marketing. Marketers are acutely aware that in the case of youth marketing, the subjects of their study are different from them. The gap between their age and that of their target can make them nervous. Believing at the outset that the target segment's behavior is inherently different from our own puts us under pressure to show them as someone not relatable to people like us.

The trap with youth marketing is that we end up treating youth as a different animal. We imagine sullen hoodlums with tattoos all over their bodies, multiple piercings, and spiky hair. We imagine them to be beings completely distant and different from us. We isolate them, then we microanalyze them, only to say "Hey, you know what? Youth likes music. And they like to hang around." But really, how different is that from what you and I like to do? Don't you and I like music too—and may be hanging around as well? It's just that our hanging around and our music may not be same as theirs. The point is that youth is not a different species, to be analyzed through *National Geographic* lenses. They are just another generation who need to be understood from their viewpoint rather than from the outside.

Bridging the Gap

Building a real youth brand in such a context calls for a change in outlook. We need to look at the world from their side up rather than looking down at them from our world. We need to embrace a frame of observation (research) that allows us to experience life, its anxieties and desires, through the eyes of youth, and we need a way of responding (brands) that become more internalized, a part of them, rather than trying to push the brands at them from the outside. If we keep our distance, observing from the outside, we remain in that space that is youthful but not necessarily youth. It's critical therefore to create a bridge for interaction between the marketer and the target segment as well as the brand and its audience.

It's also critical to see youth not as a different species but as just another generation—one that is part of a continuum of other generations and in many ways defines itself in relation to them. Subject to the same social stimuli, but responding in a different way. After all, what makes each generation of youth must be, in many ways, what didn't make the others!

Participation Labs

The first and foremost step in reaching real youth in a real way is creating a shared space between the brand and the consumer. This begins with interacting with those consumers to find insights into their lives. Consumer research must find a way to make this an interaction between equals. To start with, the research scenario in which the researcher is one talking to many has to change to the researcher as one among many.

Putting this into practice requires overcoming two big limitations. First, the normal process used for recruiting consumer groups tends to attract respondents whose frame of mind is exactly that—responding. For truly constructive participation, we need people who can participate frankly, sharing anecdotes from their lives, and who can help us create the prototype of the brand, including the product offering relevant to their lives. The second limitation pertains to the imaginative abilities and interest levels of the recruited respondents. Their commitment to the process is time- and incentive-bound; their levels of interest are correspondingly limited. We have learned that this is not the framework of interaction best suited for cocreation.

However, we have successfully run youth interaction sessions by innovating with the research process. Our key target segment was youth in the age range of 15 to 25. We decided to create what we called "participation labs" by reaching potential participants in two ways. The first route was to tap the friends-of-friends network. From the youth who we already knew socially, we built a group of friends. Their desire to participate and their degree of participation were high, as for them, it was a group time with the people they wanted to hang around with anyway. The second route was reaching out to college students by putting up posters on campus. Those interested were asked to answer certain questions designed to ascertain their ability to create and cross-connect and their desire to participate in such exercises.

We used the resulting youth participation labs to explore large life themes and hypotheses about youth's changing behavior. We also invited them to come up with product and service ideas inspired by their own life needs and experiences. Their input from the life themes went into crafting the brand message and advertising content; their product and service ideas went into the innovation funnel for new products and service proposals.

We gathered stimulus and hypothesis from general analysis of popular culture as well as our observations of the youths' behavior and of cultural trends; all of these were fed into the participation labs. Our purpose was to build on them further and finally funnel them into specifics for brand and product ideas. This allowed all the input—from the popular culture, observational hypotheses, and the issues that came up in the groups—to be churned and discussed by the youth. The output thus recorded was an insider's view of youth: what they thought and what they believed others thought of them. (See Figure 7.1.)

Figure 7.1. Youth Participation Labs.

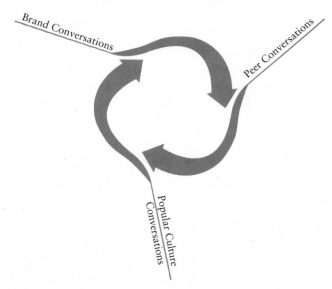

Key Drivers of Change

Youth in India today are different from their counterparts in the preceding generation, simply because they are products of different times and contexts. The experience of youth in the previous generation was characterized by rejection and frustration. The hopes that independence would lead to a golden age of opportunities were stymied by a lack of employment and rampant nepotism and favoritism. Indian youth in those times were thus flooded with angst and self-pity. After only a feeble attempt at rebellion, they bowed down to the norms of the society and succumbed to the everyday worries of life, trying to make the ends meet, and shouldering the responsibilities that various relationships demanded. The burden of getting the younger sister married, taking care of elderly parents, or looking after the wife and children domesticated the young Indian man and put him on the path to his *dharma* (one's righteous duty) from the early days of his youth.

In contrast to this, today India's youth have it pretty good. The overall rise in affluence for their parents is one big contributor to this change. But what has also changed is the fundamental approach and attitude to life. Angst has given way to action, rebellion to working the system. Youths' attitude today is to make things work for them rather than wallow in self-pity. The system and their circumstances are no longer insurmountable; youth believe they can influence these and make them work in their favor. Today youth are expressing their individuality, living their lives by their own rules, having found the means and mechanisms to do so. This is unprecedented in India.

Seen in the context of earlier Indian generations, there are distinct changes in the way today's youth in India thinks and behaves. Understanding their motivations is critical to understanding and building authentic youth products and brands in this country—brands and products that speak to youth rather than merely portray youthful imagery. Let's explore these changes and what they mean for marketing to these young Indians.

1. Discontinuous Ways for Discontinuous Desires

The most remarkable change in the youth of India today is their degree of confidence and ambition. Much has been said about the confidence and ambition of the new India in general and Indian youth specifically. There is, however, a difference in the level of confidence of Indian youth compared with that of the general population. It's worthwhile to note that this is the first generation in India born in a time of plenty. They were born to opportunities and avenues that are still quite stunning to those with a longer life experience in India. The sense of optimism felt by this generation therefore has had no reality checks. Even the current slowdown has at best shown them the possibility of economic ups and downs without really affecting them.

The preceding generations of Indians have a different outlook; they have had to make their way through times of real deprivation. The specter of bad times that could be lurking round the corner is not easily banished from their minds. As a result, although most of this generation did display a sense of personal optimism in the past decade; as much as they longed to take wing, they have always kept their feet on the ground and exercised caution. Their ever-present fear of falling has only been accentuated by the current slowdown.

The youth of India today, on the other hand, want to fly without ever looking back at the ground. They want to make bold new dreams come true. Many of these are unapologetically materialistic, like owning multiple apartments, becoming a CEO by the age of 32, and so on. Most youth have entrepreneurial ambitions to start something of their own, once they have accumulated just the right amount of experience in a regular job or their family business. The biggest difference from the preceding generation is this one's ability to experiment without fear of the consequences. They will declare, "I don't regret anything in life." Those in our participation labs told us that life is like Facebook for this generation, with multiple experiences, relationships, and parts of their life including personal and professional coming together simultaneously on one platform.

Stories of incremental growth and success do not inspire these young people. Their role models are people who have come from humble backgrounds and broke new ground in their fields. These role models may not necessarily be from their own generation, though. They are inspired by people like Dhirubhai Ambani, who rose from a humble beginning as a gas station attendant to build one of the largest empires in the country, the Reliance group. And by cricketers like Sachin Tendulkar or Irfan Pathan, or any other life story of transformation from rags to riches, from zero to hero. Most of Bollywood cinema today—as well as reality television, which has managed to capture the imagination of this generation—has done so by telling stories of dramatic transformations, not gradual progressions.

Such leaps of achievement, however, cannot be achieved through traditional, step-by-step means. Unprecedented desires call for unprecedented tactics and strategies. Today's Indian youth do not shy away from taking shortcuts or exploring multiple paths; they are ready to do whatever it takes to reach their goals. Pursuing an entrepreneurial dream is therefore far more appealing to them than holding a regular job. Passing through multiple jobs or even careers in the space of a year or managing multiple relationships is all to the good, as it works toward gathering more experience. Many of the old rules of the game are being redefined. After all, the rules of previous generations were designed to maintain a path both linear and continuous. For them discontinuity was something that needed to be managed, not created.

Today's Indian youth have charted a unique course between tradition and modernity. They are challenging many of the old tenets of the traditional Indian way of life. Whether they are unapologetically pursuing fame and money—and thereby rejecting the traditional Indian belief that money corrupts—or assaying more daring acts like cohabiting before marriage, they have taken on established beliefs and shattered them. But they are doing so cleverly, without any overt rebellion.

2. Shifting Axis of Morality

For today's youth in India, the center of morality has shifted from what is culturally appropriate to what's personally useful. What's good or what's bad is now based not on what others would say but on what you want. As the youth in our participation labs put it, "We believe in being honest, but only to ourselves." The value system for this generation is self-constructed; it's designed to work for them. For the traditional India, a value system has been something that you must live up to; for this generation, the value system is something that helps them achieve what they want. It's more a means to realize their desires than a destination in itself.

The shifting center of morality also means that much that was sacrosanct for previous generations is now being questioned. The youth of India today feel no pressure to present a social face of phony goodness—unlike previous generations, whose words and deeds were always constrained by what people might say. In fact, a bit of "being bad"—small shortcuts, some manipulation, a little greed—is actually OK with many members of this generation. One of the youth in our participation labs reiterated the old Hindi saying: "If you can't take out *ghee* [clarified butter] with a straight finger, you should use a crooked one." Which essentially means that if you can't get your work done through fair means, it's fine to use crooked ones. This tenet, traditionally seen as the reprieve of the unlawful elements of the society, seems to have become the mantra for today's young generation.

This shift is manifested in the rise of the new antihero archetype in Bollywood. The quintessential villain as he formerly existed in the Indian cinema—the repository of all that was socially evil—is dead. To fill the void, the hero of the Bollywood has turned a little gray, cutting some corners at times, not hesitating to pull a fast one to get what he needs in his path to success. There are plenty of instances of such behavior in most successful Bollywood films of recent years. *Dostana*, which was released in 2008 and grossed over Rs.85 *crores* ($17 million) worldwide, told the story of two men who pretended to be gay so they could rent the apartment of a young girl who would never rent to two young straight bachelors. Similarly, *Luck by Chance*, the story of a young guy who wants to become a Bollywood actor, has the protagonist cozying up to a much older actress because he knows that she can help him win the screen test for a movie in which her daughter has the lead role.

It's important to note that the new antihero is more clever than mean. Most of his manipulations and shortcuts are lighthearted and essentially harmless, done without any truly evil purpose.

Though there is no overt rebellion between the new value system of the youth and the entrenched social norms, there certainly is a play between the two worldviews. There are two possibilities for resolution: either the youth finds a way around things, or he agrees to toe the social line in return for a favor. For instance, he may agree to accompany his parents to a dinner with the relatives, in return for a promise that the next day he can stay out late with his friends. This is a clever barter of power, in which neither side gives away its full standing while each of them manages to get what they want.

In a culture in which following what's socially dictated had previously been the norm, acceptance of gray areas does not come easily. India today is still coming to terms with this changing axis of morality. It's a common topic of everyday conversations among the senior generation, who are partly flummoxed and largely agitated by what they call a loss of morality. Though a bit of this is beginning to be reflected in cinema and television programming, to date it has been little recognized or used by brands.

3. Seeking Partners in Crime

Compared to previous generations, the youth of India today are a generation born with, as the saying goes, a silver spoon in the mouth. Not only are they coming of age in a time that's relatively more affluent and optimistic, but they are also making the most of what they have, be that in their careers or in their relationships. These young people carry no baggage of yesterday and have no significant gaps between what they have and what they need. A consumer base so situated is a nightmare for classical marketing, which is designed chiefly to identify large need gaps in its consumers and find ways of filling them.

Youth in India today are not looking to brands to make themselves feel liberated or empowered in the way that traditional youth marketing does so adeptly. What this generation *is* seeking is a certain legitimization of their new way of life. The rules that they have written in the pursuit of their own way of life need a

subtle endorsement. After all, although they may not have completely overturned the applecart, they have certainly tweaked
the social codes to their advantage. Now they'd like brands to
endorse their value system. Not from a pedestal, but by being one
with them. By playing buddy and being a partner in crime.

Their true desire is for a relationship that's born not out of
hierarchy but from empathy. They want to hear a language, a
tone of voice, and a set of mannerisms that belong to their world,
not the generation that marketers belong to. It's almost as if
they want the brand to be a character among them rather than a
stranger trying to communicate from a distance. This is a big shift
for a culture like India, which scores high on power distance; this
is a culture in which people have always sought idols that they
can look up to and have always wanted to put those they choose
to emulate up on a pedestal. As such, most relationships in India
have been hierarchically coded. There was never a dearth of role
models; the universal desire to have one created many.

Here too change is apparent: Indian youth today don't have
one single role model. Their role model is a mishmash of various
qualities that they admire in the successful heroes of the society
or from their own personal lives. So they may admire the ability of a Sachin Tendulkar, the belief of Dhirubhai Ambani, and
the perseverance of their own parents. But above all, the youth of
today look up to themselves; they are their own role models.

Youth today are multifaceted, with many aspects to their lives
and many sides to their personalities. It's unrealistic for any brand
to play to just one of these aspects and expect to connect with
youth as a whole. Just like the human body, this generation will
instinctively reject foreign objects. It's only possible to connect to
this generation by becoming one of them. From this position, one
can enable a world of opportunities and possibilities that would
not even be visible from outside.

A New Framework for Youth Brands

One trap that youth marketers can fall into is trying to connect
with youth by saying "I am a youth brand." This might look
logical from the marketer's perspective, because you have

decided to target the youth. To the youth, however, this statement of intentions means nothing unless you connect with
what motivates them. Further, this kind of thinking leads to
advertising that projects a rather superficial image of youth—
say, two guys jumping and tossing a basketball around. In the
telecom category, for instance, it's typical to offer a "friends"
plan, and every other ad in this category shows a bunch of
youth partying at a pub or dancing in a conga line, holding
each other's backs.

Clearly marketers need to look at youth marketing in India
from a vantage point different from that used for the traditional
models of youth marketing. Most branding frameworks look for
need gaps and fit brands into them. But for Indian youth today,
rising affluence and better opportunities mean they have the
money, relationships, and job options that their senior generation
could only dream of. They look to brands not to fulfill unmet
needs but to legitimize their fulfillment. They seek brands built
on a model of partnership.

Looking at youth marketing from the viewpoint of youth
has several implications. First, as mentioned previously, the
brand must become an intrinsic part of the youth's life. Second,
the brand must find multiple ways of adding value. Think of the
brand as powering up the networked, Facebook life that youth
today are leading. This demands that marketers turn their usual
single–minded-proposition thinking on its head. A brand in
youth space cannot confine its delivery to the primary benefit
that the category offers. For example, a mobile brand for youth
cannot flourish simply by enabling voice and data connectivity,
which in a traditional marketing paradigm is its primary benefit.
The brand has to work harder, find other links in the web of the
youth's life that it can help maximize. The premise is simple: if
you want to be their friend, then you need to be able to do more
than just one thing.

The recommended model for youth brands requires considering
these fundamental shifts from the traditional models:

- From saying "I am about youth" to *being* about youth
- From a relationship of hierarchy to a relationship of partnership

- From fulfilling a need gap to legitimizing a way of life
- From a single-category benefit to multiple links in their lives

Thinking of Youth Brands as Life Links

As shown in Figure 7.2, brands today must define themselves not by filling a single need gap for the consumer, but by enabling links in youth's lives.

In this framework, as brands forge links in the lives of youth, they help them maximize their lives. The marketing focuses on not what links the brand to youth, but what the brand links within their lives. This in turn means that rather than making a singular connection between the brand and the consumer, the brand enhances multiple links in the consumer's life. Each brand therefore can deliver multiple benefits that its category can support. It's critical that, based on the brand's strengths and what the category enables, each brand chooses which links it will play and how it will do so in a fresh way.

For instance, a youth brand in the apparel space may offer peer-to-peer reviews on its latest products at the brand store, on

Figure 7.2. A New Framework for Youth Brands.

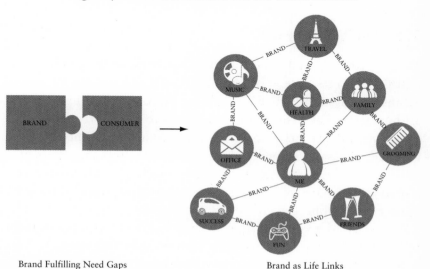

Brand Fulfilling Need Gaps   Brand as Life Links

its websites, and even through mobile phones. The brand then is tapping into not only the desire to look good but also the idea of peer shopping and helping youth link to their community and their opinions. Similarly, a snack food brand can play on youth's immersion in music and partying, enabling ways to organize better get-togethers with friends—going beyond the basic need for between-meal foods to help link together the youth's entertainment network.

With the point made that the brand should go beyond the basic delivery of the product category, note it's still important that the brand carefully choose and craft its area of play. For instance, although a mobile service brand can easily enable youth's links with entertainment, it may find it difficult to play in the area of health and fitness. And it's critical to understand the role the category itself plays in the life of youth. Apparel and fashion wear for youth may have more to do with community approval and appreciation than with just style and fit. One young girl, trying out various tops at Mango (the women's fashion brand), each time asked her mother: "Is it smart or will it look stupid?" She was more worried about what her friends would say than how the top actually looked on her. Imagine building a store that allows her to check in with her friends and get their comments while she shops.

True Blue Youth Brands

Virgin Mobile is one such attempt at building a youth brand that's true to its core. The brand has told stories that pit youth against the system, which is made up of parents, professors, and authorities. It has exhorted Indian youth to bypass the firewall of sanctions rather than try to break through it. For the first time on national television, Virgin Mobile offered storylines and characters that were not sugarcoated and socially proper. Its advertising presented stories purposefully designed to bring out some of the gray areas in the public space.

One showed a young girl pretending lesbian tendencies in front of her parents, just to manipulate them into letting her go to Goa with her boyfriend. In another, a young biker manages to bypass a hardnosed traffic cop (in the Indian context, these are often corrupt and seeking bribes) by making him talk on his mobile phone to his father. Actually, he pulls a fast one on the cops. He asks the cop to talk to his father, but he dials his friend whose number he has saved as "Papa." Still another Virgin Mobile ad showed a typical Indian government clerk falling for a faux sex hotline—implying that it's the senior generation that is perverted, despite their constant harping on the scandalous ways of today's youth.

It's not that youth's new way of life has been hidden from society. But facing it openly was a matter of social discomfort. Virgin Mobile has come out as a courageous brand, unafraid of openly addressing what's been swept under the rug by others. The brand has placed itself at an important junction in the mobile phone category, which, in the context of today's youth, is exactly on the cusp of their struggle between freedom and restrictions. The mobile phone is a compromise between parents and children whereby youth get their independence and parents get to keep tabs on them. Thus that first phone is a symbolic coming-of-age ritual, with youth negotiating their freedom from the powers that be: parents, teachers, and bosses. Virgin Mobile has positioned itself as a brand that is a partner in their crime, helping Indian youth to find their own independent space.

MTV has always positioned itself as one with youth's own viewpoint. In its first incarnation, MTV was among the initial set of brands that adapted their programming to suit the tastes of Indian youth, who liked the songs of Kishore Kumar (a popular Bollywood singer of the 70s and 80s) as much as those of Michael Jackson. MTV's positioning around "*desi* cool" (local is cool) took on the Indian belief up to that point that everything international was cool. And in an economy and an environment finally opening up, this was exactly what Indian youth were looking for—a validation of their own remixed way of life. With properties like *Bakra* (a prank show), *Fully Faltoo* (a parody of Bollywood), and the Lift Man (a character who despised MTV), the channel entered the lexicon of Indian youth from their side. MTV, which unabashedly celebrated being Indian, became a marketing case study on how to localize global brands for success in India. Keeping pace with the changing times, MTV in India is revamping, going beyond music and launching reality shows like *Splitsvilla* and *Roadies*. The brand today has competition from several other television channels, such as Channel V and Bindass, that have done a good job of connecting with the Indian youth, but nobody can take away from the fact that MTV started it all.

Being on Youth's Side, Looking Up

Simply applying unadapted Western models for building youth brands to a country like India can lead to a severe disconnect. In Western marketing models, there's an inherent assumption that the distance between the youth and senior generation is wide enough to pit the young against the old and build a brand out of this tension. In today's India, however, the tension between youth and their senior generation is of a different nature: the newfound affluence of the middle-aged is making them behave youthful in a way that threatens to crowd out the young; it's a too-close-for-comfort feeling. Thus, rather than being able to celebrate their distinct difference from the older generation, youth in India are seeking first to build some actual distance from them.

However, most research frameworks are designed to report the consumer as a third-party entity, and for most brand models, it's just another box of unmet needs. And most seasoned marketers end up analyzing youth as a separate species; their underlying assumption is that youth are really very different from who they themselves are. As a result, they end up building an image of youth who are everything that they are not—creatures constantly dancing to hip-hop and hanging around in malls.

Marketers need to create a shared space for the consumer and the brand, where both are treated as equals. The first step to bridging the gap is in the way we interact with consumers to find insights. We need to participate in their lives and make them participate in the process of creating the brand by facilitating this equal space. The "participation labs," as we call them, were thus created with youth actively involved rather than simply recruited to become subjects.

The world of Indian youth has seen fundamental changes, especially compared to the previous generations. What was sacrosanct till now has been made fluid. Their desires are discontinuous, their morality is self-assessed, and they are seeking a partner in crime rather than just fulfillment of their need gaps, which are far less significant than those of prior generations. A consumer segment like this needs a framework of brand building that is nonlinear and nonhierarchical—a brand framework designed to immerse the brand in the life web of the youth rather than plugging into it from outside.

Shifting from fulfilling needs to forging life links is a fundamental departure from traditional brand thinking. Till now, our primary preoccupation was connecting the consumer with the brand; now we must focus on how many links the brand enables in the consumer's life. We need to move beyond the central category delivery and ask ourselves: "In how many ways can my brand power my young customers' lives?" As we begin the journey of creating this bridge from brand to youth, we must keep this intention firmly in our minds.

8

SEAMLESS SAVITRIS

THE NEW INDIAN WOMAN AND NEW MARKET OPPORTUNITIES

Breaking the Internal Glass Ceiling

At a Confederation of Indian Industry (CII) conference on women in 2005, the hotly debated topic was whether there was a glass ceiling for women in the Indian social and business environment. In the midst of a daylong session of system and male bashing, the real revelation came when the women who had made it despite the odds spoke about breaking through their own *internal* glass ceiling. The strongest point made during the day was that even before the woman in India faces the external glass ceiling, she is hindered by her own diffidence. But once she manages to break through her own lack of confidence, the world and the entire system come around to work in her favor.

The urban Indian woman has, to a large extent, overcome the anxieties of social acceptance and gender insecurities. She is no longer condemned to prove her abilities solely in the realm of nurturance and selflessness. The middle-class woman today wants to be known for more than her ability to endure. She has in fact gone beyond this and reclaimed parts of her individual self. As one of them said in our consumer interaction, "I like to work, to feel that I am also worthy even if it is in a small way . . . it is my way." Stories of Indian women proving themselves on the world stage, against all odds, are commonplace today. On the Forbes 2009 list of the hundred most powerful women, India had four entries: Indra Nooyi of PepsiCo, Chanda Kochhar of ICICI Bank and Kiran Mazumdar-Shaw of Biocon, and the Congress party president, Sonia Gandhi, who, although not Indian by birth, has come to epitomize the strength and purposefulness of the modern Indian woman.

Across socioeconomic strata in India, women today have a strong desire for achievement, the desire to make something of their own lives. They are finding support in their mothers, who themselves were denied any such dreams. The story of Pooja Chopra, who was crowned Miss India World 2009, exemplifies this. The 24-year-old was brought up by her mother, Neera Chopra, with great financial and emotional difficulties, as her father had deserted them when she was young. Pooja, by sheer dint of ambition, with support from her mother, reached the doors of the Miss World 2009 competition. Mother and daughter together helped each other break their internal glass ceilings.

In a very different area, the International Olympic Committee announced the entry of women's boxing in the 2012 London Games. India is one of the countries that pushed to break the gender bar for this sport and lobbied for its inclusion. The *New York Times* ran a detailed article in August 2009 on how the Indian boxing team, preparing for the 2012 London Games, is a living example of young women determined to "punch in the big league."[1] Boxing, as the article illustrates, is more than a game for these women. Most of them come from humble family backgrounds, and boxing for them is a way to attain a middle-class life and become somebody. When they're in the ring, it's as if they're fighting not just their opponent but also their own fears of being condemned to a life of rearing cattle or children.

Whether it's sports or entertainment or even reality shows— think of Sania Mirza in tennis, Saina Nehwal in badminton, and Sourabhee Deb Verma, the winner of *Indian Idol* season four—Indian women are topping the charts in the men's world. Today's Indian woman, however, is busy creating her own identity rather than competing against her male counterparts.

The woman of today is competing with her femininity rather than against it. Unlike in earlier days, when a woman seeking acceptance at the male-dominated workplace had to groom and dress herself more like them, today's woman has found a way to be herself. She is less busy watching over her shoulder for her male counterparts, more busy watching her own steps. She has learned to use her charm and intelligence to get ahead and prefers soft power over aggression. As Deepika Padukone, a rising Bollywood star, said in one of her interviews, "New feminism isn't about being aggressive; it's about reaching the top yet being soft. It's about being you—feminine, strong and full of will power."

Dependently Independent

The women of India today feel that they are independent because of the support that they get from their spouses and parents. Their independence is symbiotically linked to their dependence on their families. A wife's relationship with her husband is a partnership; the belief that they complete each other keeps them going. This is a marked departure from the nature of marriage as it was, say, a generation ago, when it was loaded heavily in favor of the husband. This maturity in the relationship comes with the woman's confidence that her ability is no longer in question. In many families today, women are net contributors to the family's finances, much to the relief of the husband who was for so long burdened to be the chief wage earner.

The new-age adage seems to be suggesting, "Behind every successful woman is a man." That's certainly true of Mary Kom, India's most acclaimed boxer, who holds the record of winning four gold medals since the inception of the women's world championships in 2001. Kom had kept her boxing a secret from her family until she won a state championship in 2000. However, once they learned of it, she was constantly under pressure from her father and members of the community to quit, especially after she married. But Kom's husband, a former soccer player, turned out to be a big support for her career. It's because of him that she is gearing up for the 2012 Olympics, despite having two children. Stories like those of Kom and her husband are getting to be common for Indian families of today, but the nature of that support keeps changing. Sometimes it's about the husband teaching her how to ride a Scooty; in other cases, it's about how he encourages her to start her own venture.

This shift in thinking has found its way into the popular culture as well. Whereas female protagonists in earlier movies needed to be rescued by their men, today they are a credible helping hand in fighting the villains. In *Dilwale Dulhania Le Jayenge* ("The Lover Will Take the Bride"), released in 1995, the female protagonist, played by Kajol, is a demure Indian girl who waits to be rescued by her knight in shining armor, played by Shahrukh Khan. Whereas in *Rab Ne Bana Di Jodi* ("A Match Made by God"), released in 2008, the female protagonist, played by Anushka Sharma, thrashes her harassers black and blue, while her husband, played by Shahrukh Khan, rides the bike. Even in television reality shows, in which many married women participate nowadays, the women express profuse thanks to their husbands for supporting them. The husbands are shown waving from the audience, happy to be on television even if only for their wives.

In the pursuit of her independence, the Indian woman is still very connected to her relationships, drawing energy from them and sharing the rewards. The mothers of contemporary young Indian women are an important source of inspiration, exhorting their daughters to go forth and make their dreams come true. Though young Indian women's connections with their mothers are deep, they fervently hope that they will be able to go beyond what their mothers were able to accomplish. "My mum didn't have the freedom to do what she believed in and I have enough freedom to do what I believe in," is how one of them put it during our consumer interactions. These superwomen of today hope to have it all: along with finding career fulfillment, becoming mothers and wives as good as their own mothers have been.

The Cultural Middle Point

In the modern Indian household, the woman is like a semipermeable membrane. On one side she wants to expose her family to newer influences; on the other, she feels she must safeguard the value system of the home. She is the one who champions the need to buy a computer for the children, but at the same time insists that all family members sit down together at dinner. Modern Indian women are both the roots in tradition and the wings to modernity. They exemplify the cultural midpoint in today's India.

This also means that while the woman's core values are strong and intact, the execution can sometimes be flexible. So when it comes to tradition, the woman of today stays true to the belief but evaluates the rituals on their merits. For instance, she may believe in the idea of *Karva Chauth*—the traditional Hindu festival when married women fast for a long life for their husbands. But she may not believe in going all day without food and water. Her own flexible version of the ritual does not in any way mean a dilution of her belief. Similarly, she believes in giving respect to elders, but she also believes that respect doesn't mean following blindly everything that they say.

Tradition in India has always been quite flexible for men, but it has never given women similar room to play. The choices were stark, either/or. Women in past generations therefore had to choose: either career or marriage, either the guy she loved or her own family. Thus, for women who valued independence, rebellion was the only way out. For the urban Indian woman today, the choices need not be so stark. Independence for her has meant freedom to choose what she wants rather than having to choose between the options that the society forces on her. She can choose to work and therefore postpone marriage for some time. She may also leave her job to stay at home and bring up children if she so wishes. Being independent and being a housewife are not mutually exclusive, just as having a career and raising a family are no longer either/or choices. The mix between tradition and modernity, social and personal choice, individual and family is more balanced for the Indian woman of today.

Finding Herself

The archetypical Indian woman lived a life of borrowed identities. She was always known in relation to somebody else (male): her father, her husband, her son, and her brother. The Indian woman of

today desires to move out of the men's shadow and find some fulfillment of her own. The Bollywood movie *Honeymoon Travels*,
released in 2007, showed one of its protagonists, played by
Dia Mirza, running away with her love interest, played by Arjun
Rampal, while threatening her husband at gunpoint not to stop
them. In another movie, *Life in a Metro*, a character played
by Shilpa Shetty is well married with a six-year-old daughter.
Burdened by a life of daily chores and not being able to get much
from her busy husband, she falls in love with a struggling theatre artist, though she stops herself before she crosses the line.
It's not that movies around the subject of a woman's desire have
not been made in India before, but most of them stayed in the
world of critical acclaim rather than finding a mainstream audience. Though at times a bit exaggerated (in the typical Bollywood
style), the cinema of today is capturing the reality of the urban
Indian woman seeking to find her true self.

The search for herself, however, is not always a sexual or
a romantic one. Even a simple act of pampering herself with a
beauty parlor treatment and not feeling guilty about it is a mile-
stone. This came out in our mother-daughter interactions, when
a 50-year-old mother said, "During my days, if I had to go to
the parlor, it was to look good for a special occasion. Shopping
for clothes and accessories was rare and there had to be a good
reason." Whereas her 25-year-old daughter said matter-of-factly,
"I go to the parlor when I want to feel good about myself and
indulge myself with a facial, pedicure, and manicure. I shop whenever I feel like it or see something I really like." The younger Indian
woman is recognizing her own personal self, giving her individual
desires a chance.

Women in India have always been taught to be self-sacrificing
and to put others first. The source of joy has traditionally been
in keeping others in the family happy. In our consumer interactions with mother-daughter pairs, it was interesting to hear how
mothers said that it made them happy to see that their children
were doing well, the husband was staying in good health, and the
family was well taken care of. Whereas the daughters would say,
"I have a responsibility to myself and my happiness; if I am happy,
I can make the people I care about happy." Although the focus on

keeping others happy hasn't gone away, her personal happiness has finally found priority in her scheme of things.

Spending as you wish and not having to ask for permission to make small purchases is a small but really significant act of self-empowerment. In that sense, the modern retail formats have unintentionally contributed to the urban Indian woman's sense of empowerment. Pushing the cart through the aisles of the modern store, choosing the best for her family and some especially for herself, she escapes from the drudgery of her chores for an honored traditional cause: the family. The decisions that she makes in these aisles are hers alone, and she knows that she has the implicit approval of her husband. A marked improvement over previous generations, when all a wife could do was hand over a list to her husband and hope he would get her what she had asked for.

Money Is a Facilitator

For the Indian woman today, wishing to seamlessly facilitate the many parts of her life, money plays a critical role. She understands that money smoothes out a lot of unpleasantness in life and can be used to spark fun in the family. If she is working outside the home, she uses money power to make small things happen for the family—perhaps, in part, to make up for her day-long absence. For women not working away from home, the desire to keep contributing to the finances of the household is extremely high. Many of them have either considered or are actively involved in enterprises like running a boutique, selling financial products such as insurance, or working part time from home. In both the cases, money is helping her express her love: her ability to earn it and spend it makes her a better mother.

Wealth, of course, is a joint resource for the family. Her role in saving and building assets of whatever size is a story that she tells with much pride. Whether it's a subscription to a regular savings product like an insurance policy or goading her husband to invest in a property for their life after retirement, the woman of the house is often the chief initiator. The income of the family in most cases thus has a household ownership. As one woman said in our consumer interaction, "It's not your money or my money; it belongs to both of us." Wealth is owned jointly and is seen as a product of teamwork.

However, money is also a sensitive issue, especially when it is earned by the woman of the house. While she initiates wealth creation and indulges in small expenditures for self and family, the "authorized signatory" of the house is still the man. The link between a man's ego and the control of money is well understood by today's Indian woman. She knows that he is OK with her going out and working as long as he feels in control overall. Lest it disturb the general equilibrium of the home, it's better to leave the controls in his hands. There is no harm in making him the signatory; ultimately it's her plans that he signs off on.

A Sense of "Complementality"

The idea of the family in modern urban India is moving from *sukhi parivar* (prosperity) to *khushi parivar* (fun). Thus the family is an entity geared toward fun and growth. The traditional idea of a family in India was an extended one—married couples lived with their parents, children grew up largely on their own—each family developed organically, unplanned, simply happening. The modern-day nuclear family is much more consciously crafted, with carefully selected partners and deliberately planned children. Parenting today is a serious exercise. The purpose of the traditional family was a happy coexistence; the purpose of today's family is growth of the individuals. Adding value to each other and making more of whatever they have are the motivations that drive this unit. Powered by EMIs (estimated monthly installments) and supplementary incomes, this family is being run to maximize its resources.

Being together is not what defines this family—being there for each other does. Traditionally, in the extended family, there was always somebody around and in times of need, such as medical emergencies, there were family members who could fill in for the absent husband. But these days it's no longer OK for the husband to be away on critical occasions—even if it is as small as, say, the child's first parent-teacher meeting. Parents of past generations sometimes had to grope for the name of one of their own children (there were so many of them to remember!) whereas parents of today are expected to even remember the names of their children's friends. Being there for each other when needed is more important for today's family than merely living together. The Indian family today is about complementing each other's mentality—a sense that we can call "complementality."

The family of today is knitted together more by fun than by responsibility. The earlier skills of adjusting to and coping with many varied relationships have been replaced by those of managing, solving, and enabling. Children don't just bring hope; they are active family members who play a critical role in most key decisions. *Badon se pooch kar* (asking the elders) has been replaced by *bachchon se pooch kar* (asking the children). Chores must be made less ritualistic and more attractive by injecting play and discovery. This family is brought together by malls and gaming zones and weekend outings. Happiness is a legitimate objective here.

The facilitator of this nuclear family, the woman of today, partners her husband in this venture. Her role in the relationship has changed from being a subordinate to being more of an equal. She now goes to the railway station to pick up the visiting parents-in-law if the husband is stuck at work. She anticipates his failures and makes up for them. She can go out to pick up that pastry that her husband has promised their son but will inevitably forget to bring. She lets him present it so that he looks good as a father. She remembers to pick up gifts for his dad's and best friends' birthdays. The husband, for his part, recognizes her role and doesn't mind preparing the breakfast if she is busy packing their children's school bags. If she is experimenting with a new recipe at home and finds a critical ingredient missing, he is the one who rushes out to get it for her—to help ensure that her experiment is successful.

Seamless but Stretched

The woman in India traditionally lived her life in stages. Her life before marriage was one stage. Her dreams, desires, and relationships from this life seldom made it to the next stage, which was her married life after the wedding. Similarly, once she had children, that became her full-time occupation and the husband took a backseat. The woman of today, however, is no longer playing purely singular roles; she lives in several life stages simultaneously. She is today a working mother, her son's best friend, and her husband's girlfriend, and she still manages to keep in touch with her school friends. Her life flows seamlessly between her yesterday and today, career and personal life, family and self. She is stretching herself to make one role continuous with another.

The area of influence of the modern Indian woman has clearly expanded beyond the hearth. The shift out of her parental home is not that permanent anymore, as in most cases, connections remain strong and frequent. Her past and present social circles amalgamate to create a new larger whole. The relationship with her husband is one of real support in all areas, not just an emotional one. She is adept at managing the house, banking, and other utility needs. She is her husband's office counselor and her children's home tutor.

As a result, the much used and abused marketing payoff of "appreciation from husband" on which many FMCG brands built their fortunes is no longer a woman's key desire. The woman of today is seeking to be in the social spotlight. She no longer laments the apathy of her busy husband. Her source of appreciation is her immediate social circle, whether it's the teacher at her kid's school who appreciates her parenting or the woman in the neighborhood who asks for her opinion on make-up techniques or the Residents Welfare Society, which invites her to choreograph their cultural show. She is expanding her area of impact beyond the boundaries of the home and is seeking appreciation on the social stage.

But the superwoman is stretched, trying to maintain the seamless connections among various parts of her life. In her attempt to give 100 percent to everything, she is inevitably being pulled in all directions. The earlier equation perhaps was easier, as she was supposed to perform in the home while the husband played his outside role. With a merger of roles, the pressures are high, as she tries to be competent across multiple theaters of life. Brands are recognizing this stretch and speaking to women

about it. For example, Horlicks, the milk supplement traditionally meant for children and old people, has launched Women's
Horlicks. The brand observes that she is the one who is missing
from her long "things to do" list and exhorts her to include herself—
"Because your body needs you, too."

Marketing to Stereotypes

Marketing and advertising, however, has made its own use of
stereotypes when it comes to addressing the woman of today. The
most common theme is the woman taking on the man's domain.
In the world of Fair & Lovely, for instance, she gets to fulfill her
dreams of becoming a cricket commentator, which is traditionally
the exclusive dominion of men. In another advertisement for the
same brand, her beauty inspires her suitor to measure up to her
by losing weight. But the brand has always been interpreted in
the context of the man. Whether it's the Nivea Visage imagery of
a successful city girl taking on the boardroom or Max New York
Life Insurance showing successful women as pilots, the larger
discourse is still centered on victories in the man's world. Very
little of this takes note of the shifting measure of a woman's self-
appraisal, whereby she is watching her own steps more than the
shoulders of her male counterparts.

Much of the marketing portrayal of the Indian woman is still
the traditional stereotype: the woman busy keeping her family and
husband happy. The Kellogg's Special K campaign for women is
centered on the idea of the woman having to lose weight for the
husband's office party, and Taaza tea celebrates her appearance on
television for her tasty *dum aloo* recipe. Though brands like
Sunsilk, with their "Life can't wait" campaign, and Dabur Vatika
hair oil, showing free-spirited women playing football and riding
a bike, depict women losing their inhibitions and having fun, the
portrayal of the new Indian woman essentially goes no further.

The other code that has been liberally used is that of role reversal,
with the woman shown pursuing the man. Most of these portrayals
are in categories that basically target men. For instance, advertising for Bolero, a midsized SUV from Mahindra, shows two
model-gorgeous women on water scooters flirtatiously circling a

guy with his Bolero (although it's not entirely clear whether the women are attracted to the SUV or the man). Tata's Indica Xeta is pitched with a group of girls inviting a hunk to help them rub on sun-tan lotion. Sumo Grande, an MUV from Tata, shows a woman in a car chasing the good-looking owner-driver and disappointed to finally see he has a little son sitting next to him. Clearly, this is an image of women intended to sell to men rather than to women.

The Indian market is beginning to see some innovations in terms of new products designed specifically for women, like new formulations of corn flakes from Kellogg's and insurance policies from Bajaj Allianz. The image portrayed, however, lags behind the new attitude of Indian women. Most of the ads push an assertive, almost masculine archetype in an attempt to make women look like the stronger sex. Others play on women's anxiety about not doing enough for themselves, commanding them to make themselves on a priority. This patronizing tone is out of touch; today's Indian woman does make herself a high priority.

New Woman, New Opportunities

The fact that the Indian woman is moving beyond traditional roles means that the marketing of products and services to her must move beyond them as well. Traditionally, she has been the target for FMCG players who have appealed to her largely as a mother and a wife, for various products from milk additives to detergents to cooking oil. Even personal care and beauty products spoke to her need to look good for her husband.

Some marketers have woken up to the opportunity; indeed, now women are being targeted overtly in categories where they formerly had no recognized role to play. ICICI Prudential, the largest insurance player in India, is one of the prominent ones to make this shift in its communication. The insurance brand had long highlighted the promise of the man to be there for his wife and family. They successfully used the cultural idea of *sindoor*, which is symbolic of a man's marriage vows to the woman. One of ICICI Pru's recent campaigns, however, has used the woman of the family as the catalyst for making an insurance purchase. She insists that the husband sign the insurance papers, not because she is worried about herself, but because being insured means a tension-free life for the husband. The brand has managed to capture the changing equation between husband and wife, clearly showing her role in lightening his burden. The light-hearted banter between the husband and the wife, in which she almost calls him stupid, reflects the security in the relationship.

Traditionally in India, while the woman was seen as the manager of the house, financial matters were clearly the man's domain. Thus finance brands here have largely spoken to the provider archetype in man. Now marketing is shifting, speaking to the woman, the facilitator of his life. A campaign by Kotak Bank is based on the observation that husbands will always be care-less with money; they will leave bigger tips at restaurants and be generous when it comes to collecting the change. The brand then speaks to the woman of the house, exhorting her to take care of the finances so that together they can live a carefree life.

The change of focus, however, is not just in terms of shifts in the communication target for categories such as finance. In the last few years, the Indian market has seen several products and services developed and targeted directly at women. Women, for instance, constitute 29 percent of the entire two-wheeler market. The women's scooter segment has seen several new launches in the past few years, with every two-wheeler manufacturer joining the fray. The advertising discourse in the category has also under-lined the shift of power in favor of women. With taglines like "Why should boys have all the fun?" the category is capitalizing on the changing place of women in India.

It's common today to see advertising for institutes such as NIIT, the largest player in IT education, being led by a woman's face. Tata has launched a second career internship program for women who opted out of an active career after becoming mothers and are eager to return to work. Started as a strategy of building a high-quality talent pool at minimum cost, the program attracted 300,000 resumes from Mumbai and Bangalore in the first five days of the advertising campaign and some 30,000 hits to the website.[2] Education for careers in the aviation industry, such as flight atten-dant, is also in high demand. Several institutes, such as Frankfinn,

AHA, and Avalon, now have a network across India, reaching smaller cities and towns.

Even in familiar women's segments, such as personal care and fashion, there are new enhanced energies. The personal care segment in India is seeing a lot of action at the premium end, with brands such as Neutrogena and L'Oreal targeting the new independent Indian woman. Dabur, which has traditionally played in the mainstream segment of the market, has entered the premium end with a skin care line called Uveda. Similarly, areas such as women's formal wear are beginning to look significant for brands like Arrow, which launched its women's line in 2009. According to a 2008 report by RNCOS, an industry research firm, the women's apparel market in India was anticipated to grow at a compounded annual growth rate (CAGR) of 17 percent to cross Rs.61,000 *crores* ($13 billion) by 2010.[3]

The Indian woman today has come a long way. Savitri, the mythological archetype of the Indian woman, was celebrated for her dedication to her husband. As the legend that is a part of the epic *Mahabharata* goes, she walked the path of death behind her husband Satyavan and persuaded Yama, the god of death, to return her husband to life. The modern-day Savitri is defined not so much by her dedication to her husband but more by her active support. Today's Indian woman is standing up for her husband, her family, and for herself. She is an active support and contributor, not just a passive shoulder to lean on. She adds to the household economy, independently accomplishes tasks that need to be done beyond the home, and she can counsel her husband on office politics. In her desire to be seamless between her various avatars though, the wannabe superwoman is being stretched to her limits. Marketers need to applaud her for her accomplishments and find ways to make life easier for her.

9

SMALL IS BIG

THE GROWTH OF THE SMALL-TOWN
AND RURAL MARKETS

Charged with Potential

"India lives in its villages"—so said Mahatma Gandhi. It is now well known in the marketing and business communities that the potential of India lies beyond its top metropolitan areas and those at the top of the income pyramid. Small-town and rural India are emerging as the next fertile ground not only for consumption but also for talent. Much of the growth across several categories in the Indian economy is coming from these regions. It's certainly not on the strength of the urban areas alone that India posted a GDP growth rate of 5.8 percent in the last quarter of the fiscal year 2008–2009, compared with expectations of a less than 5 percent growth rate. The savior of the Indian economy in recent times of global depression has been its domestic economy, powered to a large extent by agriculture, which grew 2.7 percent during the last quarter of the fiscal year 2008–2009 while manufacturing growth turned negative at 1.4 percent.[1]

The increase in rural purchasing power is reflected in rural growth in a number of categories. For example, for the fiscal year 2009 (April 2008 through March 2009), rural volume growth for fast-moving consumer goods (FMCG) was estimated to be 5 to

12 percent higher than urban growth in many other categories.[2] Already, India's telecom sector is looking to these areas for its sustained growth. By the end of the first quarter of 2009, the number of mobile subscribers from rural India had surged past the 100-million mark. According to the Telecom Regulatory Authority of India (TRAI), this translates into a growth of 18 percent over the last quarter of 2008.[3] Industry estimates say that 70 percent of all new subscribers of mobile telephony will come from rural areas.[4]

All indicators of income and consumption suggest that the rural and small-town regions of India are poised to power a new economic boom. With an estimated 72 percent of the total households in India, the rural market comprises roughly 720 million customers. The size is meaningful because it's backed by income. The total income in rural India is expected to grow at a CAGR of 12 percent, from around $220 billion in 2004–2005 to $425 billion by 2010–2011. The number of rural households using banking services and credit cards—about 42 million—actually outnumbers their 27 million urban counterparts. Similarly, rural India has some 41 million Kisan credit cardholders, compared with 22 million card users in urban markets.[5] In terms of their potential, many small towns are higher on the Household Potential Index (HPI) than their metro counterparts. Based on the data of *Indian Readership Survey (IRS),* HPI indicates the amount of disposable income and purchasing power of a household. The mean index for towns with populations of fewer than 500,000 in states such as Goa, Punjab, Himachal Pradesh, and Kerala stands at 24 points, higher than the all-India average of 22.[6]

Take, for example Titan, the watch manufacturing venture of the Tata Group. Fifty percent of its sales comes from the top 10 towns while 35 percent comes from towns ranked eleventh to one hundredth.[7] Titan has launched a new line of plastic watches called "Super Fiber" as a part of their mass-market brand Sonata. Not surprisingly for a product aimed at the new customer segment, the entire Super Fiber line is priced below $10. The company expects it to play a key role in doubling Sonata's sales from 5 million watches a year at present to 10 million watches per year, over the next three years.[8]

Titan is not the only brand innovating for this market; ITC has done an extensive experiment with e-Choupal, an IT-enabled platform for agricultural information and buying and selling of agricultural produce. Nokia has launched Nokia Life Tools, a range of agriculture, education, and entertainment services designed especially for consumers in small towns and rural areas. There are many other examples of innovations and initiatives especially designed to tap the rural markets. Godrej launched its soaps in smaller 50-gram packs, Coca-Cola supplied low-cost iceboxes to make up for the lack of the reliable electric supply required for refrigerators, and Philips innovated with a low-cost smokeless stove in their pursuit of the hinterland market. Clearly, the rural and small-town Indian market is simmering with potential.

Marketers are well aware of the need to innovate their products and services to capture the attention and meet the needs of rural markets. But India A (the urban affluent India), which markets to India B (the rural high-potential India), unfortunately has a stereo-typical understanding of this world. The quintessential rural ad done by marketers in Mumbai shows a turbaned farmer sitting on a tractor, with his wife in a yellow top and blue *salwaar* (loose pajama-like trousers), amid green rice-paddy fields—the typical Mumbai conception of rural India. Mumbai has remained too far from Midnapur (a small town in West Bengal), not just physically but also mentally. But the forces of change that have affected our lives in urban India have affected rural India as well. So it's critical to understand how the world of small-town and rural India is trans-forming. It's easy to assume that these consumers are changing in much the same way as urban consumers—easy, but not necessarily accurate.

The New Small-Town India

Chak De! India ("Go For It, India!"), released in 2007, told the story of 16 small-town Indian girls, each of them a state hockey champion, coming together to win the world hockey cham-pionship. The coach, Kabir Khan (played by Shahrukh Khan), steered his team of 16 state champions, each with her own idio-syncrasies and typical small-town rawness, to win the world championship. As the Indian national hockey team triumphed in the world championship, the Indian audience cheered and clapped, seeing a little bit of their own selves in the underdogs turned victors. The *Chak De! India* story is indeed the story of small-town India and its ambitions and talents winning on the world stage.

Closer to reality, Mahendra Singh Dhoni, the poster boy of Indian cricket, is the first captain who does not come from any of the major metropolitan areas. Dhoni comes from Ranchi in Jharkhand. This is not just Dhoni's story; more than half of the Indian cricket team today is powered by small-town performers such as R. P. Singh, Virender Sehwag, and Irfan Pathan. It's especially interesting because cricket was adopted by Indians as the game of the *burra sahibs* (the British colonizers). Long after India gained independence, cricket continued to be dominated by clubs and old boys' networks from the same colleges belonging to cities such as Bombay, Madras, and Delhi. The infiltration into this elite game by the raw talent from the hinterlands is a telling story of how small-town India is hitting the big time.

The small-town invasion is not limited to the world of cricket. The 2008 Beijing Olympics saw a trio of Indian boxers—Vijender Singh, Akhil Kumar, and Jitender Kumar—reaching the quarter-finals. Vijender Singh went on to make history by winning a bronze medal—the first-ever Olympic medal awarded to an Indian boxer. Although India's athletes winning medals at Olympics is certainly big news in itself, the bigger news is that all three of these boxers come from Bhiwani, a sleepy town in India's northern Haryana state, some 150 kilometers northwest of Delhi.

Reality shows, like *Indian Idol*, are also attracting small-town performers; a large number of its finalists coming from Tier 2 cities. In fact, the winners of the 2008 and 2009 seasons of *Indian Idol* have been from small towns. Prashant Tamang, who won the third season, and Sourabhee Debbarma, who won the fourth season, are from Darjeeling and Agartala respectively. The scene in Bollywood is similar. Its reigning heroine, Priyanka Chopra, comes from Bareilly, a small town in Uttar Pradesh; the up-and-coming actress Kangana Ranaut comes from Chandigarh in Punjab. Indian talent opportunities in television and cinema are being captured by small-town India.

It is said that small-town Indian youth are hungrier to make a success of what they have set out to achieve. Shishir Hattangadi, a former cricketer, said on CNN-IBN's *Face the Nation* program on small-town Indians, "If you see youngsters in metros, they always have an alternative. If they think a certain profession is not working for them, they will choose an alternative. However, small-towners do not have that luxury. They choose one profession and they know that this is their aim and focus and that they have to go and get it."[9] Now, finally, this small-town ambition is finding an outlet. Whether it's in the form of reality talent shows or an MBA degree or a job in the aviation sector as an airhostess—small-town India today is finding its own escape route, rather than being condemned to a life of struggle.

The Power Shift: From India Shining to Bharat Nirman

The power shift to the small towns and rural areas of India is not only for its business and talent potential but also for its electoral clout. The Bhartiya Janta party (BJP), which ran the national government from 1999 to 2004, approached the 2004 elections on the proposition of "India Shining." India Shining celebrated the boom and progress that the Indian economy was then going through. It got the votes of the urban audience, but the BJP suffered a huge defeat at the hands of the opposing Congress party, which went into the elections as the champion of the *aam aadmi* (the common man). Looking back, the outcome was predictable. In the general "feel good" atmosphere of overall economic progress, someone forgot to check how the other India was feeling about it all. The BJP's campaign of India Shining was salt in the wounds of those who had experienced no tangible benefits from the growth—and the election results bore this out.

Congress, which benefited from the BJP's blindness to the greater India out there and failure to make them feel included, has clearly learned the lessons. Throughout its subsequent five-year term and into its second term after winning a majority in the 2009 elections, the Congress followed a policy of inclusive growth. Congress government's latest initiative is Bharat Nirman (Building India), intended as a four-year business plan for rural

infrastructure. As stated on its website (http://www.bharatnirman
.gov.in/), Bharat Nirman aims to unlock potential, equalize
opportunity, and make rural India the new growth opportunity.

For some time now the rural areas and small towns of India
have lived with a sense of angst, of being ignored and denied
the opportunities that urban India has had access to. If only
they had access to these opportunities, rural residents feel, they
could transform their lives as well. They are well aware, through
the media, of the seductive new possibilities of consumption
and opportunities for earning a livelihood. But they have found
no real access to these high-paying jobs and alluring consumer
goods. Thus there is a feeling of denial and unfair treatment at
the hands of a system run by the privileged. Regional political
parties have capitalized on these injured feelings in a big way,
stepping up to champion the cause of these ignored masses.

The Bahujan Samaj party (BSP), led by its President Mayawati,
vows to fight for the rights of the majority (*bahujan*). Their view
is that the majority in India, which comprises the lower castes,
have been the victims of the system run by the upper-caste Hindus.
In the 2007 Uttar Pradesh state assembly elections, BSP became
the first party since 1991 to gain a clear majority. Supported by the
underprivileged classes, Mayawati has been the chief minister of
Uttar Pradesh for four terms as of this writing.

Similarly, Mamta Banerjee of the Trinamool Congress (grass-
roots Congress) party is known for her opposition to Special
Economic Zones and Industrialization in West Bengal, which she
contends are detrimental to agriculturalists and laborers. Her
party, which singlehandedly forced the Tata Group's Nano project out of West Bengal, performed extremely well in the 2009
parliamentary elections, gaining 19 seats. West Bengal has traditionally been the stronghold of the Communist party. Trinamool
Congress's 2009 performance is considered the best performance
by any opposition party in the state since the beginning of the
Communist regime.

Their ideologies can be debated, but the growing success of
the Bahujan Samaj and Trinamool Congress parties highlights the
feeling of exclusion in the small towns and rural India. These parties have come to power because they promised to stand up for

the larger India who felt nobody cared for them. The desire of those in this segment of Indian society to be heard, to be talked about, and to be a part of the larger plan is evident in the rise of these regional forces. The Indians who always came second and were treated much like the lesser sibling, are suddenly finding power of all kinds turning in their favor—economic and political as well as personal. If their display of immense talent on various fronts is not evidence enough, then their increasing social clout certainly is.

Urban versus Small Town versus Rural

The lines differentiating the demographics between urban, small-town and rural India are quite fixed. But in terms of mindset, there really is an urban mindset and a rural-and-small-town mindset. This is not to suggest that there are no differences between what constitutes the small-town India and what constitutes rural India—the truth is that among the small towns are various tier cities that differ quite markedly from each other. Overall, however, the mindsets of the rural areas and the small towns have far more in common and are distinct from the urban metro mindset.

It's possible to study small-town India and rural India as one continuum; the differences emerge only at the ends of the continuum, with a greater common area in between. Our analysis of both as a whole is appropriate at an aggregate level. The billionaires of small towns such as Coimbatore and the Mercedes buyers of small-town Punjab are certainly interesting, but they are anomalous data points, not mainstream phenomena that can explain a larger mindset or cultural shift.

Achievement Driven Youth

The story of small-town India going out and winning on the national stage is an impressive one. There are, however, significant changes going on "back home," in the life of the small towns and rural areas. Though the changes so evident in the urban areas have touched this part of India, such change is more strongly tempered with continuity of tradition in rural India than it is in the urban India. The pervasive nature of this fine balance between changes in aspirations and continuity of tradition is evident as a running theme in most of the movies made for this audience.

The achievement and ambition that characterize the over-all mood of India today are also the key preoccupation of rural Indian youth. Desire is high, especially among the younger ones, to stand out and be seen as changing with the times. They are worried about being branded as *gaonwalla* (rural—and hence uncivilized). Most of them therefore aspire to find nonagricultural occupations and are keen on acquiring vocational skills. The desire for achievement is interwoven with the quest for social recognition. Jobs in the army and with the government are seen as bringing respectability along with long-term safety and stability.

Given their history of oppression by the powerful in the system, these people put a premium on jobs that confer power. Thus jobs such as those with the Indian Administrative Services (IAS), which urban youth no longer favor as they once did, are still attractive to rural India. In the 2006 civil service exam, for instance, most students in the top 20 were from rural UP, Bihar, and South India. The quintessential hero of the Bhojpuri cinema (a regional language cinema in parts of north-central and eastern India), for instance, is a police officer. The police uniform is the symbol of having arrived in the world. In the film *Daroga Babu* ("Police Inspector"), the protagonist is going back to the village to meet his folks. But he is all dressed up in his official uniform and driving his police Jeep. When asked by his love interest, he confesses that going back to the village like this will make his family and friends proud.

The desire for achievement and progress is well underscored in the cinema created for rural India. In *Ganga*, a movie starring Ravi Kishan (a Bhojpuri actor), the retailers from the town come out to give him a contract for supplying 4,000 liters of milk every day and even pay him an advance so he can acquire the buffaloes. Elsewhere in the film, the couple makes a business of selling *litti* (a local dish of Bihar) in London. As depicted in Bhojpuri cinema, a mix of native ingenuity and new opportunities is creating a new spirit of optimism in the rural world.

Unlike earlier times, though, opportunities are not only presented for those leaving the village. They are also coming to the village, albeit in smaller doses. Many villages in India have benefitted from the boom in urban retailing and the developing market for agricultural-based products. McCain Foods, the world's largest producer of French fries and other potato products, has undertaken contract farming of potatoes on around 1,000 acres in areas such as Deesa, Vijapur, Palanpur, Himmatnagar, and Anand, to the benefit of some 400 farmers in north and central Gujarat.[10] Reliance, which has already rolled out 177 Reliance Fresh stores across major towns in 11 states, has drawn up plans for a presence in 6,000 *mandi* (wholesale market) towns, with 1,600 rural business hubs to service them.[11] Add to this the efforts by many other food and retail players, including the much-discussed e-Choupal initiative of ITC, and it's clear that the benefits of a prospering economy are beginning to trickle down to the Indian farmer, who is suddenly in a greater demand.

Pride in Roots

The new generation of rural India is desperate to embrace modernity—and to them, modernity seems to come in the guise of "urbanness." To achieve this, it's essential that they shed the villager image and look unrural. They are determined to defy all negative associations with a rural life, such as disheveled hair, an unshaven face, an untucked shirt, and so on. On special occasions, they make it a point to use personal enhancement products such as perfumes. Friends from the city and movies are the key sources from which rural youth learn about fashion fads. They feel that speaking in English makes them look cool, so they try to speak what little English they know.

The desire to don urban clothes and behavior doesn't in any way mean that the small towns and rural areas of India are willing to let go of their roots. In fact, they feel strongly that they are the real keepers of tradition. Rootedness is a critical part of their sense of identity—perhaps the only thing that sets them apart from their privileged counterparts of urban India. Across the range of regional language movies, situations are set up to validate the goodness of everything that's rural and rooted. In *Daroga Babu*, for instance, the protagonist favors *litti chokha* (the local specialty) over burgers and pizza. In one sequence in the film *Sasoora Bada Paisawalla* ("My Rich Father-In-Law"), a city girl abuses a coolie in English for dropping her bags. Our hero confronts the girl, asking her not to treat other people as insects just because she has had a little education. The setup deliberately contrasts the goodness of rural character with urban insensitivity.

The village simpleton versus the city slicker is a long-standing set piece in Indian cinema. Whether reality or myth, the stereotype of warm-hearted, selfless rural people still seems to warm the hearts of rural India. In the movie *Vivah*, Amrita Rao plays a young girl from a small-town Madhupur. An orphan, mistreated by her aunt, she always responds to her with kindness. Similarly, in *Daroga Babu* the hero refuses to accept a bribe; in *Ganga*, the protagonist defends the untouchables. These themes of inherent goodness still have their charm for the rural audience, though they have vanished from the movies made for the urban audience. The urban scene depicted today is more about manipulation, meanness, and finding your way no matter what.

On a similar note, the family in rural India is still considered something to sacrifice for, at least in principle. Respect for elders and their responsibility is a virtue highly eulogized. All successes and achievements are celebrated by touching the feet of elders, the ritual for seeking blessings. In the movie *Ganga*, the protagonist takes responsibility for his mother even when he himself is in dire circumstances. The sanctity of the family unit is one of the foremost values that rural India wants to hold on to in times of change. In this part of the country, the individual is still less important than the collective.

Individuality Finds Expression

For some time now marketers have proceeded on the assumption that all purchases in rural India are household purchases. This pattern, however, is changing. Individual choices in personal care products are emerging in this market. It's not unusual to find different brands of the same category under one roof, like

Colgate toothpaste for the young and Dabur Lal Dant Manjan [tooth powder] for the parents. Consumers are becoming familiar with various products and can distinguish among various kinds— whitening toothpaste for shine, herbal toothpaste for protection, and so on. Their preferences, too, are becoming clear; they will tell you confidently that this toothpowder is rough and that particular oil is too strong.

Media exposure and a brush with the outside world by way of schools and colleges, which are generally in nearby cities, are bringing a sense of individuality to rural India. The preference for personal care products is influenced by what they have seen in city shops. Their selection of personal care products is expanding to include more specific offerings, with a general movement from say, basic moisturizing creams such as Hans (a common brand in rural India) to special-purpose creams such as No Marks and Fair & Lovely. Men too are becoming appearance-conscious: fairness brands such as Fair & Handsome have found a significant following among these consumers.

Standing out from the rest and being recognized is a critical motivation, especially for the young. Sunita Gogoi, an Assamese participant in the dance reality show *Dance India Dance* on Zee television, confessed that her biggest motivation was to prove to the skeptics back home that it was worth her while to put time and effort into perfecting her dance. Even in the remote villages today, people feel the need to stand out and be noticed. Much of this, however, is limited to dressing differently and exercising individual choice in personal care products.

Rural Women: Transformation Within Boundaries

Their newfound access to the same brands and products used by their urban counterparts is allowing rural Indian women to feel on a par with them. Today they not only see the latest consumer choices on television but also have access to a larger range of those products than ever before. When they visit their relatives in the city, they find them using the same brands of shampoo or toothpaste that they use in the village. Although they still fear being perceived as backward in their outlook, incidents like these make them feel that they too are keeping up. Hindustan Unilever, Dabur, Cavin Kare, Godrej, and other such brands seem to be enabling this bridging of the gap between the two worlds, even if only through the means of consumer goods.

The other big change for the rural Indian woman is that today her opinion in household matters counts. Whether it's about the future of the children, the upkeep of the house, or even her own choice in personal care products, the woman of the rural India now is entitled to have her say. She is proud that she has a higher degree of engagement in household affairs. With her husband, too, her role is more one of a partner than just a subordinate. She provides the emotional strength in the relationship—advising him to leave the work worries outside, putting him at ease. The husband in turn is not shy of doing his share to an unprecedented degree; for example, getting the children ready for dinner while she is cooking the meal.

The younger, unmarried rural women have a more confident and bold attitude. Their talk is unselfconscious and not self-censored at every step for fear of consequences. At this stage in their lives, career choices such as becoming a doctor or an engineer are wide open; so is the prospect of moving to the city for higher education. Once they marry, however, that boldness is reined in. Now they must think more carefully about what they say and do. Their desire to do something outside the household role lingers, but those youthful dreams of becoming a doctor or engineer are replaced by more modest ones of becoming a teacher or a beautician. These women have a strong desire to hone and nurture their talents; they are not happy just to be great cooks at home or good homemakers. They may wish to learn *kathak*, the classical Indian dance form originated in northern India, or play the *dholak* (the double-headed hand-drum), or take up painting. Even knowing how to apply make-up skillfully and practice good grooming is considered a skill.

The rural woman may have to fit her aspirations within the boundaries of the society and her relationships, but she still wants to exercise creativity within these boundaries. Her entrepreneurial streak is commendable in itself and is encouraged by the husband and the family elders. She is eager to do something on her own, from being a seamstress or a neighborhood beautician, to contributing to cottage industry initiatives such as making *papad* (a thin crispy flatbread). She takes pride in her ability to make more out of her limited means. This is a true rendition of the traditional idea of the Indian woman, who is referred to as *Annapurna,* which literally means "full of food." In Hinduism, *Annapurna* is a goddess of fertility and stands for bountifulness. Traditionally the woman of the India is supposed to bring bounty to the household; her ability to make more from of the scarce resources at hand is seen as her key asset. The rural woman of today's India is no less than a modern *Annapurana.*

The Need to Shine

Conventional marketing wisdom has dictated that less-evolved markets be played more on functionality and problem-solving platforms. Many traditional brands targeting such markets have therefore taken these positions. However, consumers in these markets are evolving. They are being exposed to new stimuli, not only through media but also through interactions with the outside world. In the personal care category, for instance, the rural consumer's expectation is shifting from basic problem-solving benefits (such as a cure for bleeding in gums) to a greater emphasis on visible appearance benefits (such as shiny teeth). Promises of increased self-confidence and compliments in a social context that a consumer gains from visible benefits, such as shiny teeth and glowing skin, are no longer the sole preserve of urban consumers; rural India wants them too.

Small-town and rural India today no longer have modest desires. Quite the contrary: these are consumers acutely aware of their handicaps. Hence they fight that much harder. They know that that they have inner self-esteem but lack the polish of their urban counterparts. They score high on ability, but fall short in matters of personal comportment. They feel vulnerable to losing out on the brink of opportunity for a simple lack of polish. Commonly, in the small towns and rural areas those who aspire to pass the coveted civil services examination ultimately move to a bigger city for interview coaching. The Indian civil service entrance test

puts a strong emphasis on the personality interview, which inevitably tilts the odds in favor of the more polished urban dwellers.
Small-town and rural aspirants therefore work harder to compensate for this lack through extra coaching. The colloquial saying is
that "whatever be the brand of shoes, the polish has to be Cherry
Blossom." This is to say that your basics may be really sound,
but you still need a polish to take you the rest of the way.

All of this makes the need for "look-good benefits a high priority for these consumers. They need props to help them shine
with confidence. In their brands and products they seek support
for escaping the "rural" badge and finding urban success. They
are looking for such support in just about every aspect of their
lives. Most brands have realized, consciously or otherwise, that
rural Indians today aspire to succeed and to do so with flair. Across
categories, therefore, propositions for the brands targeted at this
segment have moved to the space of either appreciation or achievement. Whether it's Fair & Lovely or Chick shampoo or Pond's
Dreamflower talcum powder, all are playing up benefits in the
area of "looking good" more than just "doing good."

Take, for example, Dabur Lal Dant Manjan, a historical brand
of red toothpowder not just for Dabur but also for any Indian
who was around during the Doordarshan era (the period dominated
by the government-run television channel). "*Raju, tumhaare
daant toh motiyon jaise chamak rahe hain*" ("Raju, your teeth
are shining like pearls") is a well-remembered advertising slogan.
Over the years, Dabur Lal Dant Manjan got credit from its consumers for its ability to keep their teeth problem-free. Consumers
considered it a rooted, "son of the soil" brand, ensuring both
physically strong teeth and, by inference, the solidity of the rural
Indian. But that was then. As consumers began upgrading to
modern products such as toothpastes and gels, the toothpowder
category stagnated—and so did the brand.

In an attempt to bring the brand in line with the changing
desires of rural consumers, Dabur Lal Dant Manjan has attempted
to reposition itself to straddle its "doing good" benefits with some
"looking good" benefits. The television commercial is woven
around a character who is academically brilliant and would pass
all written tests with flying colors. But when it comes to interviews,

he invariably gets rejected because of poor oral hygiene. Dabur Lal Dant Manjan is shown as the way to teeth that shine with the glow of health and thereby help him attain the good things in life—not just the interview but also the girl. By depicting success on a stage outside the rural setting, the brand has broken out of its "son of the soil" stereotype. Dabur Lal Dant Manjan, in its attempt at reinvention on modern terms, underscores the changing aspirations of Indian consumers and an increasing need to sell appearance benefits in rural India.

A Trajectory of Its Own

Life in rural India is certainly changing. It's critical to understand, however, what exactly has changed—and how much. We generally are more comfortable attributing changes like the rise of ambition and individuality to urban consumers than to the rural ones. It's not easy to accept that much of these changes are actually percolating down to what's been popularly called the bottom of the pyramid. However, if we refuse to recognize the reality of these changes, we will continue to operate based on our entrenched stereotypes.

One of the stereotypical portrayals of rural India is the "son of the soil" characterization. For a long time, brands trying to appeal to this audience have taken this route, with direct references to the solidity of rural roots. But the "son of the soil" has been transformed. Today he is modern in outlook, though rooted in values. The archetype of a rural guy loaded with naïveté and goodness is fast fading from reality. The real person out there is trying hard not to get labeled as a *gaonwalla*—the uncivilized rural inhabitant. We need to get comfortable with the fact that rural consumers can be progressive too.

In the rural context, the idea of strength has always been interpreted as physical. So the default practice with most rural brands has been to use celebrities with a popular image as action heroes, such as Sunny Deol and Sunil Shetty. Take, for example, the oral care category in the rural context, which is stuck in the physicality of strength. Most storylines are about being able to open the cold drink bottle or being able to bite into a hard fruit as a demonstration of strong teeth. However, even in the rural context the idea of strength has moved on from physical to mental strength. Today it's about being smart in your actions and resilient in your thinking, about using brains and not just brawn.

The universal assumption that the rural world is in awe of the urban world and wants to become exactly like them is simplistic. For most of rural India, the old awe of the outside world has been vanquished by access to it. The city is not that far away any more. It's a place they visit every now and then for studying, working, and even shopping. The idea of going out and making your mark in the urban theater too is quite probable today. Moreover, it's not only about going out; opportunities are coming home to small towns and rural areas. Images of an urban life appear on television every day, rendering them commonplace. Also, access to brands and products in personal care, mobile telephones, and many other categories have made the two realms, once so far apart, look rather similar. Rural India thus no longer lives in awe of urban India; these consumers simply want to maximize all the new opportunities that they now have access to.

Rural and small town India have their own trajectory of growth; they are not following the urban idea. In reality, rural India is growing on its own path, expanding its area of play in its own unique way. Life in rural India is not fully stuck in yesterday, nor has it crossed over to a completely new way of life. It's a world with real individual motivations, not all of which are replicas of those in the urban world.

THREE GENERATIONS, ONE BIG MARKET

OPPORTUNITIES IN A NEW SEGMENTATION OF INDIA

Between Homogeneity and Hypersegmentation

India is big and India is young. Its size and its demographics, together with its growth potential, have made it a fashionable market. Marketers from around the world and within India are betting big on these two aspects of the country, even more so in the recent global economic downturn. But these are also the two most critical characteristics of India that every marketer must examine carefully and truly understand, in order to succeed in this country. India is big, but is India one huge, homogeneous market? Or are there different segments in India that have distinct behavior patterns? India is young, but is youth the only marketable population in India? If not, then aren't we missing a piece of the picture? Most of the marketing and advertising in India today is designed for the young mindset. With the entire country being made to feel young, what's happening to those who are actually young?

The problem with India as a market is in many ways similar to the problem with India as a tourist attraction. A few years ago, a global internet survey on India as a tourist destination revealed that in most parts of the world, the country enjoyed a high level of awareness and appeal. But most of the people who would have liked to come to India never got around to making a plan, because of India's daunting complexity. Although India was attractive, its vastness and diversity offered no easy entry points: how to get in, where to go, and how long a trip to make. For marketers, India's one-billion-plus consumer base looks similar: attractive but complex, with no direct entrées into feasible segments, and little specific demographics beyond big, young, and growing.

Not that there haven't been attempts to segment the India opportunity into smaller bites. Several segmentation approaches have been propounded, and many studies have been conducted by marketers, researchers, and advertising agencies. But most of these segmentation methods, rather than solving the problem of complexity, end up adding to it. Segmentation approaches based on the belief that there are many Indias within one India suggest several permutations and combinations leading to infinite consumer segments. Other research efforts bunch Indians into segments based on a certain pattern in their reported behavior. This doesn't really tell us whether the different behavior patterns are from different people or the same people at different times and moods. Most segmentation approaches thus either hypersegment India or manufacture segments better suited to PowerPoint presentations than to the real world.

The value of India as a market is still in its massive size. To hypersegment India is to undermine the value of the opportunity. We need a way to segment India that unlocks a greater opportunity, rather than thinly slicing up what we already know. A way that unveils what lies beneath the surface of this big, young, and growing country. A way that enables us to better grasp its diverse elements.

Mainstream Myopia

The flavor of India today is young. Every brand and business in the country is asking itself "Are we positioned appropriately for the young India?" Those who realize they aren't, quickly gear up for a brand makeover. It's no wonder that many a recent advertising agency brief comes from an old, fuddy-duddy brand seeking a transformation into an image that's young, energetic, and contemporary. One prime example is the public sector banks, at least three of which (State Bank of India, Bank of Baroda, and Canara Bank) have attempted to add youthfulness to their brand personality in the past few years.

The advertising landscape in India today predominantly features young faces, with the older generation either eased out or playing a supporting role at best. Ask any media planner in the country—age 25 to 24 is the most universal target audience definition for the mainstream brands that the planner works with. If we could take advertising and brand targeting as a serious indicator of the demographic spread of India, we would safely conclude that everybody in India is between the ages of 25 and 44.

A look at the demographics of the country, however, shatters this myth. According to the *Indian Readership Survey 2010 (Quarter 1)*, there are about 168 million people in India in the age bracket of 45 and older, of which 27 million live in urban areas and belong to the top three socioeconomic classes (SEC A, B, and C). This then appears to be a segment that has both size and potential and can by no means be dismissed. Our single-minded focus on the 25 to 44 age group, however, has meant that those 45 and older are never addressed with any seriousness. This begs several questions. Does everything in India need to be young? Are we ignoring a market at the higher end of the age spectrum in India?

The picture looks incomplete at the other end of the age spectrum as well, because the 500 million Indians under age 25 are also ignored. The mindset and needs of those under 25 are indisputably distinct from those around 44—especially because the times in which the two age groups have grown up are culturally so different. Considering that there are 207 million Indians between 15 and 24, of which 25 million live in urban areas and belong to the top three socioeconomic classes, we are missing out on another significant segment of the market. What are we doing to leverage this age group?

Most marketing in India suffers from a mainstream myopia focused only on that magical 25 to 44 segment. Although this certainly is the most significant and perhaps most profitable segment in the country, we seem to be chasing the young mindset but forgetting the youth. And in our zest for youthfulness, we have lost sight of the older segments and mindsets—even though their numbers and their pockets both indicate a highly profitable segment. We desperately need a new set of segmentation lenses to correct this myopic vision.

A New Basis for Segmenting India

Epochal events shape the mindset of a nation and fundamentally define the mindsets of the generations that live through them. Such epochal sociocultural events can thus be used as variables for segmenting the country into different mindsets. Two such epochal events have impacted India and the way it thinks in a big way. The first one is, of course, the political independence of the former British colony in the late 1940s, which also led to a rather painful partition into two countries, India and Pakistan. The second was the economic liberalization of India—which, of even greater importance than the opening up of the Indian economy, has opened up the minds of Indians.

The political independence of India, though attained after much struggle, turned out to be a mixed bag. Independence brought the implicit promise of a brighter future, kindling hopes of employment, prosperity, and other fruits of self-governance. But the joy of independence came with the sorrows of separation. Partition meant destabilization for many people who had to leave well-settled lives overnight and move to a new country, a new land—becoming refugees in their own country.

Those uprooted by partition worked hard to rebuild their lives but in the process grew inherently suspicious about their future and destiny. Unfortunately, the hopes born of the political independence of the country remained just that—hopes. Generations of Indians post-independence struggled with unemployment, scarcity, and a system that failed them at every turn. Faced with hardships and obstacles, they grew up trying to make more of the little that they had, finding a way where none existed, and adapting to whatever life had to offer.

Hurt by onslaughts from outside, India as a nation also drew inward. It tried following policies of self-sufficiency and *swadeshi*—promoting indigenous produce. Socialist theory influenced most of the economic policies. Politically, India followed a policy of nonalignment with both of the power blocs of the cold war. It played an active role in the Non-Aligned Movement (NAM) and tried to create regional cooperation through the South Asian Association for Regional Cooperation (SAARC). So, in the decades that followed political independence, India as a nation and its people turned inward, learned to hold back, and became increasingly skeptical about the future.

This self-imposed isolation was eventually overcome by the country's economic liberalization. This reopening made way not only for influences to come into India but also for Indian ideas, talent, and enterprise to reach out to the world—and the opportunity for India to become a world player in the knowledge economy. Suddenly ability, not capital, became the foremost currency in the country. As a result, today this nation and its people, who nearly surrendered to fatalism, are discovering that they can actually transform their being through the sheer dint of their ability.

The string of changes sparked by the economic reforms is leading to a deeper sociocultural transformation of India. Never before have India and its people been so profoundly changed in such a short period of time. This makes the current times in India and its current generations very special. The momentum of change is molding different generations in different ways. The central age group, for instance, is busy making the best of the new world of shining opportunities while trying to balance it with the traditions of their childhoods. The younger generation, on the other hand, born in times of abundance, are not similarly bound by history; their only allegiance is to today and consequently to themselves.

The political independence and partition of India and the economic liberalization of the country have shaped the mindsets of the people of those times with impacts beyond their immediate periods of influence. These generations have not only their own distinct worldviews but also distinct consumption patterns.

Recognizing political independence and partition and economic liberalization as two epochal events, we can see India as a combination of three mindsets or segments.

A Mélange of Three Mindsets

India today is a unique mélange. Based on the age at which these events of critical influence caught them, Indians can be segmented into three key mindsets: the Partition Generation, those born into the times of political independence and partition; the Transition Generation, those born into the times of economic liberalization; and the No-Strings Generation, those born into the times of affluence and post–economic liberalization. Details are shown in Figure 10.1.

The oldest members of the Partition Generation—a group that is today aged 45 to 64—were around one year old when the political independence and partition took place in 1947 and the youngest of their cohort were born 18 years later, in 1965. They number 168 million in India today. Of these, 27 million live in urban India and belong to the top 3 socioeconomic classes. Restricting this to the top 35 cities, they number 13 million.

Figure 10.1. Proposed Mindset Segmentation of Indian Consumers.

Segments	Age in 2010	Age at Liberalization (1991)	Total Population (millions)	Urban Population; SEC A, B, C (millions)
Partition Generation	45–64	26–45	168	27
Transition Generation	25–44	6–25	350	56
No-Strings Generation	15–24	0–5	207	29

Indian Readership Survey, Quarter 1, 2010. SEC is the socioeconomic classification of India, which classifies its urban population based on education and occupation parameters.

The Transition Generation is 25 to 44 years old; the oldest were 25 and the youngest six when India liberalized its economy in 1991. This means that their formative years were marked by the peak of the changes that the economic liberalization brought to India. They constitute a population of 350 million in India today. Of these, 56 million live in urban India and belong to the top three socioeconomic classes. Restricting this to the top 35 cities, they number 26 million.

The No-Strings Generation is now aged 15 to 24; they were born in a liberalized India to relatively more affluent parents and in more optimistic times. They have a population of 207 million in India today. Of these, 29 million live in urban India and belong to the top three socioeconomic classes. In the top 35 cities, they number 14 million.

Potential at Two Ends of the Spectrum

With about 27 million people aged 45 to 64 and 29 million aged 15 to 24 in urban India within the top three socioeconomic classes, there is certainly more potential at both ends of the age spectrum than is currently being leveraged by marketers in their focus on the 25 to 44 age range (see Figure 10.2). This potential at both ends of the age spectrum seems hidden from marketers. We need to pull back and see the full picture. There are three Indias in India. Three generations in this one big market. Understanding this unique mix has implications for business targeting, brand propositions, and language as well as product innovation pipelines.

It is true that India is changing rapidly, in both economic and social terms. It's also true that the overall flavor of the market is young and dynamic. But to be able to understand the impact of change, it's critical to understand where these different population segments are coming from—which determines their different responses to the change stimulus. Their distinctive worldviews and mindsets create distinct consumption patterns and expectations from brands and products.

Figure 10.2. Potential at Two Ends of the Age Spectrum.

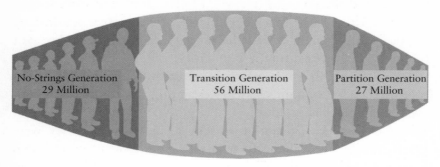

*Urban Population; SEC A, B, C (millions); Indian
Readership Survey, Quarter 1, 2010.*

The Partition Generation: Cautious Opening Up

Manoj Kumar, a veteran Bollywood actor of the 60s and 70s, was in the news not long ago for several reasons. He was honored with a lifetime achievement award at the 14th *Annual Star Screen Award* function. And there was controversy, as he had been caricatured in the Bollywood blockbuster film *Om Shanti Om* and felt quite upset about it.

Manoj Kumar, it's important to understand, made a respectable name for himself as Mr. Bharat (Bharat is the Hindi term for India), starring in and directing films that were a commentary on the struggle of the everyday common man in post-independence India. One of his biggest hits, *Roti Kapda Aur Makaan* ("Food, Clothing, and Shelter"), dealt with the turmoil of a middle-class Indian caught between principles and poverty on one side and a system flourishing in corruption on the other. *Roti Kapda Aur Makaan* embodied the struggle of the Partition Generation for whom the independence dream failed to bring the promise of prosperity. The movie was the highest grosser of 1974.

Manoj Kumar is the hero who epitomizes the principled patriotism of the Partition Generation. Yet a Bollywood blockbuster movie made in twenty-first-century India poked fun at a particular pose that he was famous for and everybody took it in jest, till the actor himself took offense. Not that *Om Shanti Om*, which is actually a spoof on Bollywood and is replete with self-referential jokes, did so deliberately. But it spotlights the differences among the three generations. At one end is the Partition Generation, who have lived all their lives to earn and command a certain sense of respect from the society. In the middle is the Transition Generation, members of which sat in the jury of the Star Screen Awards and decided to honor what this veteran actor had done for India through his movies. At the other end is the No-Strings Generation, for whom *Om Shanti Om* is just a *masala* movie—a spiced-up entertainment, giving them light-hearted fun. Why, they wonder, would anyone take offense?

To understand why, we need to explore four key themes that amplify the worldview and consumption behavior of the Partition Generation.

1. Held Back But Not Holding Back

The Partition Generation carries baggage that it has been unable to shed completely. The struggle with scarcity, the pain of separation from a well-established life, and the failure of the independence dream have all scarred them. They witnessed a gradual moral degradation in public life as people in power grew prosperous through not-so-proper use of that power. At a personal level too they feel a sense of loss, as they never had a definitive life plan to work with. As one said in one of our interactions, "We had no goals; we just studied and passed examinations in the hope that we [would] get a job, stand up on our feet, and be able to support our family."

This has sown in them an inherent suspicion of the system and their own fate, a fear that something will go wrong, something will give way. The shadow of history holds back their lives. This is the generation that in family discussions in their living rooms today questions the role of a multinational corporation like Frito-Lay in setting up potato chip factories in India. They fail to understand why we need foreign manufacturers for something as banal as potato chips, which every household can roll in its kitchen. This generation is generally skeptical of many modern phenomena: niche careers, women's independence, postponed marriages, meteoric career growth, and the government's personal interest in increasing privatization. One of our Partition Generation consumers put it this way: "I don't know what these girls of today are trying to prove by smoking cigarettes in front of us."

They have realized, however, that some changes are better accepted than resisted. "If you will not bend, you will get blown away," said one of them. Though they are skeptical of the change, they also feel its seduction, and they want to participate in it. As Sheilu Sreenivasn, founder and president of Dignity Foundation, put it in an article titled "Life Begins at 60" (*Times of India*, February 2008), "Having spent the better part of their lives fulfilling their responsibilities toward parents and children, it is now time to turn their attention to themselves. For a generation that saved wisely, finances are not an issue either."[1]

One of the key areas of spending for this generation is vacations, which includes trips to religious as well as exotic places. Kesari Tours, one of the leading tour operators of India, runs a special tour for elders called "Second Innings." They have identified this segment as a high-opportunity one, as many of the elderly are cash rich and many of them also receive these tours as gifts from their kids. Another big growth area is that of housing developed with sensitivity to the needs of this generation. LIC Care Homes have planned a model retirement village for the financially sound. The units are designed to be self-contained, with a central kitchen, smooth-operating elevators, and wheelchair-accessible bathrooms. There is a provision that the leased property can be passed on to a beneficiary on the death of the resident. Built on a five- to seven-acre complex, the village offers a gym, walking track, a library, a community center, and a kitchen, in addition to medical facilities. The first has been built in Bangalore, and LIC Housing Finance has plans to open others in Bhubaneswar and Jaipur.[2]

The value system that this generation grew up with holds them back, but the avenues that they can see around them pull them forward. Whether forced by circumstances or seduced by new possibilities, this generation is gradually opening up to many of the new influences of today's India. Many of them, for instance, have taken avidly to computers and the Internet, either to stay in touch with their children who have moved abroad or to log onto matrimonial sites such as shaadi.com, searching for suitable life partners for their children. But they are cautious in their exploration of these new things, and more often than not, it's a selective adaptation rather than an absolute adoption.

2. Desire for Permanence

The Partition Generation plays for keeps, whether it's relationships, investments, furniture, cars, or moral values. They confess to an unqualified commitment to their rituals and traditions. "We do it exactly the same way that we used to do it," said one of them in our interactions.

When N. R. Narayana Murthy, born in the year before partition and a cofounder of Infosys, spoke at Wharton's MBA commencement in 2001, he exhorted the new graduates to be trustworthy, create a support system in their families, live with dignity, and strive to make a difference to their society. It's remarkable how Narayana Murthy, who has built a world-class organization in the ever-changing digital space, champions the permanence of this value system for himself and others.

Nothing better illustrates this generation's desire for permanence than the UTI fiasco in the early years of this century. UTI is an asset management company with public ownership, making it a quasi-governmental company. UTI's US-64 scheme was probably the most popular mutual fund among Indian small investors; many of them put all their lifetime savings, including their retirement funds, into the scheme. In 2001, the scheme ran into some financial trouble and all transactions related to US-64 were frozen. There is no big surprise in a mutual fund running into trouble; the real surprise was the dismay and denial of its investors, who protested that it was a fund owned by the government—so how could the performance of a government-owned fund fluctuate?

Their early experience with the instability of life and the unpredictability of tomorrow has made the Partition Generation seek stability in every aspect of life. They are the ones still pushing their children to uphold the traditional institutions such as marriage. No wonder they form a large portion of the traffic on the matrimonial websites. The Partition Generation still has a high regard for traditional, stable brands such as Tata, Birlas, and SBI. They park their money in the government-run Public Provident Fund and bank fixed deposits; they are major contributors, emotionally and sometimes monetarily, in the average 32-year-old's buying of a house on loan. With its values of stability and security, the Partition Generation thus acts as an anchor. They preserve a long-term perspective, whether in consumption or in the culture.

3. A High Regard for Functionality

The Partition Generation clearly prefers substance over style. Packaging for them is exactly that—packaging, which they feel is there, more often than not, to make up for the lack of substance in what's packed inside. Brands are more about an assurance of quality and durability than about self-expression and larger meanings. The Partition Generation thus consumes categories rather than brands. Within categories, however, they will seek brands that give them the best value and an assurance of good quality.

This generation has lived with a lack of many amenities. Many of the categories of today's lifestyle are new for them. Thus what they often want is simply a membership in the category rather than a choice of brands. Access brands, which provide access to certain categories with high value but perhaps plain imagery, do a good job of selling functionality to this generation. These brands, such as Kakaji Namkeen (the local brand of wafers and other Indian snacks), which provide value substitutes for rather expensive-looking brands in the same category, such as Lay's, speak effectively to this mindset. These brands carry enough assurance of the quality and quantity that this generation demands; at the same time, they appropriately spend very little in building imagery that is useless fluff for this generation.

The Partition Generation, in contrast to the others, is driven more by the functional value of the category than the emotional imagery of the brand. This attitude comes largely from the traditional Indian thinking that regarded simplicity as the greatest virtue. Some of the owners of large Indian businesses and senior bureaucrats can easily be found living a very simple life, wearing unfashionable clothes and preferring home food to any exotic cuisine. There's a stark difference between their lifestyle and thinking and those of the succeeding generation, for whom a life of luxury is not about extravagance but about comfort and enjoyable experiences.

4. Community as a Key Support

When we asked them to point out the key values that they lived by, the Partition Generation spoke fondly about "creating respect" for themselves in society. This theme came out with surprising consistency and passion across our interactions with them. It appears that community, for this generation, is both what they live with and what they compare themselves to. For instance, social status or showing off is a way of life for the Partition Generation, especially in many areas of the North, in and around Delhi. Most of these people had to start their lives from scratch as refugees, post-partition. As life progressed, they grew in desire to signal to their community how far they have come from where they started. Status, or "show-off" as it's popularly referred to, is nothing less than a marker of success for this generation.

Community is an important support for the Partition Generation. Take, for example, the Udipi restaurants that line the roads of Mumbai, serving up cheap yet delicious south Indian fare. The very concept of Udipi restaurants is born out of a community need. When hordes of people from the southern part of India came to Mumbai, they realized that while all of them worked throughout the day, they needed someone to cook food for them to eat in the evening. The Udipi restaurants derive their name from the native town of most of these migrants. In Mumbai today, Udipi restaurants are a category unto themselves, and to this day the community acts as an essential support for those working in the restaurant, by supporting them with start-up capital to branch out and open an Udipi joint of their own.

For the Partition Generation, community has been the ultimate recourse for all kinds of recommendations or connections, in the government or outside it. Being able to obtain some *sifaarish*—a personal word from a person of power to get things done—is a subject of much pride. The community continues to be a source of opinion and recommendation on issues ranging from marriages to consumer products. The concept of peer pressure carries a very teenage connotation, but the concept of "community counsel" would be the exact counterpart of peer pressure for the Partition Generation. The views of people in the extended family and those around in the community are very critical for this segment. It's no wonder that multilevel marketing companies such as Amway and Avon have been very successful in capitalizing on the highly connected social network that this generation has. Several insurance businesses are also tapping into the "community counsel" appetite of this generation by recruiting financial advisors from within their ranks.

Transition Generation: Heading to Tomorrow, Bringing Yesterday Along

Recent years have seen a trend of remakes and remixes in the Indian cinema and the music scene. Never before have so many old Indian classics been remade on such a grand scale, nor so many old songs remixed to become chartbusters. Essentially, they have taken an old storyline or lyrics and rerendered them with a lot of gloss and contemporary styles and references. Though the content is from older times, the mood is today's.

Devdas, a tragic story of a self-destructive hero and his unrequited love, was remade for the third time in 2002. In this new version, the rather sad story of *Devdas* played out through magnificent *havelis* (mansions), colorful costumes, and choreographed dance sequences. This modern version of the tragic love story was told in a rather celebratory tone and evoked fewer emotions of pathos and tragedy than of opulence and beauty. The glossy version of *Devdas* turned out to be highly successful.

The popular trend of remakes and remixes pretty much exemplifies the state and the desires of the Transition Generation. As a generation brought up by the Partition Generation, they have been imbued with all the values that their parents lived by.

However, as a generation that was at its peak when the winds of economic liberalization began to blow, this generation has seen a new world of opportunities open up right before their eyes. They certainly want to embrace the new, but they do not wish to leave yesterday behind. They want to sing the lyrics of yesterday to the tunes of today. The Transition Generation seeks to minimize the conflict of transition. They want to fly high with their feet on the ground. They want to sail far while still anchored in the harbor. This desire for anchored adventurism guides the worldview and consumption behavior of the Transition Generation.

Here are some of their key life principles and the implications for brands and businesses.

1. Letting Go

Boogie Woogie, one of the longest-running dance shows on Indian television, ran a mothers' championship. For possibly the first time in Indian history, middle-class Indian housewives traded their aprons for dance shoes and competed on national television, with their parental in-laws clapping in the audience. India seems to be witnessing a dance revolution. The sheer number of television shows based on dance has gone up dramatically. Some have even managed to attract serious personalities from public life, such as the national coach of the Indian hockey team and a popular chef, to the dance floor. Dance today has become an integral part of everyday life; no party is complete without a DJ. Shaking a leg has never come so easily to Indians who had for so long mastered the art of self-restraint. One of the biggest differences between the Transition Generation and the Partition Generation is this ability to shed inhibitions, to let go.

The Transition Generation is learning to be flexible. The hierarchies and structures in their relationships are loosening. Whether it's the boss-subordinate relationship or father-son interaction, there are certainly many more high fives in this generation than in any before them. They are learning that it's OK to indulge themselves sometimes and that enjoyment is not a sin. In many extended family households today, in which the Transition Generation lives together with the Partition Generation, an implicit agreement seems to be at work. It's fine today for the younger ones to consume alcohol or non-vegetarian food in their own room, even though previous generations never consumed any of these, for religious or other reasons. It's said that where there's a will, there's a way—and this generation is certainly finding a way to peacefully coexist.

As the Transition Generation is shedding its inhibitions socially, there's a similar trend in their consumption behavior as well. Letting go means they're increasingly willing to make discretionary expenditures. This is the most targeted age range for brands across products and services. Seduced by new choices and supported by rising household income, the Transition Generation is clearly relishing the joys of consumption.

2. Chasing Tomorrow

The world has opened up for this generation in many ways. Life today offers many more choices. From career options to brands within categories, the Transition Generation is being seduced by the possibilities of what they can do and what they can become. There was a time when their parents waited a year for the delivery of the humble Bajaj scooter. Today, they are being chased and courted every day by marketers of loans, credit cards, and mobile phone services. The Transition Generation seems to love the seduction, and they are quickly learning to demand more of everything. Having seen the constraints that their parents lived with, this generation wants to achieve everything that the Partition Generation desired but could not get.

But life in the fast lane is not all smooth for the Transition Generation. Having seen an unprecedented boom followed by a slowing economy, they live with a constant fear of failure. Just as their successes belong to them, so do their failures. They know that if they can't make it, they have nobody but themselves to blame. In our consumer interactions, one of them said, "No doubt life is becoming better, but so have the demands, and we are always running short of resources to meet all of them." Yet their belief in a better tomorrow has not waned. That's a story that this generation is still ready to buy.

3. Reconciling the Dilemma of Change

The Transition Generation is embracing the new world that's opening up to them. But even as the doors of tomorrow are being flung open, they can hear the doors of tradition closing behind them. They don't want to leave behind the past in order to move ahead; they want to nourish the practices of yesterday with the resources of today. They want to celebrate their traditions and festivals on a larger scale, with more lights, more colors, and better clothes—now that they can afford to do so.

"When I got married, I told my wife that my mother does not keep well; since then she has taken good care of my mother, and I am happy about this." So said one consumer from the Transition Generation when describing his relationship with his wife. For this generation, the relationships of today are entwined with those from yesterday. They want continuity between past and future. One of the key images that a Transition Generation group chose to describe their life was that of a father-son duo giving shape to clay on a potter's wheel. This to them symbolized their passing on of values and nurturance that they received from their parents to the next generation.

Thus the market for repackaged tradition is booming in India. An interesting case is the category of Chyawanprash, an Ayurvedic health supplement traditionally used for revitalizing health and youthfulness. From a moribund category, Chyawanprash grew by 3.8 percent in November 2003, up from a negative 18.7 percent recorded during October 2003.[3] This success has to be attributed to the efforts of brands such as Dabur, which took a fresh look and positioned this traditional immunity potion as an antidote to modern-day stress. Dabur Chyawanprash used Bollywood celebrity Amitabh Bachchan in its communication to rejuvenate the category. The contemporary version of Dabur Chayawanprash packs in the same goodness of tradition but in much glossier jars and is now also available in chocolate flavor for kids.

In its fear of losing the goodness of tradition, the Transition Generation is lapping up every bit of it. Just give it a modern, glossy twist. Not surprisingly, "sexy" Ayurveda, whether in the form of toiletries like soaps and shampoos or services like massage therapies and spas, is emerging as a big segment in India. But nothing epitomizes the success of repackaged tradition better than Fabindia. Founded in 1960 by John Bissell as a showcase of India's craft and handloom traditions, Fabindia cuts the hand-loomed fabrics of local craftsmen into many fashionable items, including wraparounds for women and short shirts for men. The brand is an icon of "Indian cool" and has gone from strength to strength. Fabindia planned to expand to 250 stores by 2010 and reported US$70 million sales in 2009.[4]

4. Credit/Debit Living

Sandwiched between two worlds always, the Transition Generation lives its life in a credit/debit mode. They are caught in a constant battle to reconcile the opposites that govern their lives. There is often a conflict between, say, choosing career growth and moving out of the home town or settling for a not-so-hot career choice and staying with the parents. Between falling in love and worrying about how good a daughter-in-law she will turn out to be. Between giving in to consumption desires for shopping, entertainment, and eating out and worrying about a dwindling bank balance.

Much of the behavior of the Transition Generation is thus com-pensatory in nature—compensating for the debits in life with an equivalent credit or vice versa. For every vacation to an exotic location, one trip is planned to the hometown. This is their way of ensuring that the next generation gets to experience time with cous-ins and the extended family. One of the consumers we met with, explained the need for trips to the home town: "We used to have so much fun in outdoor activities such as playing cricket and fly-ing kites, visiting relatives and celebrating festivals such as Diwali with them; today's kids are glued to the TV and the computer." The debit/credit principle is used extensively by Transition Generation mothers, who feel that feeding traditional food is akin to transfer-ring traditions: "We allow them to eat fast food such as burgers and pizza in the evening to the extent that they agree to eat *roti* and *dal* [the traditional platter of Indian bread and pulses] at dinner."

Thus the market for guilt and compensations for it is growing among the Transition Generation. *Taare Zameen Par* ("Like Stars on Earth"), a 2007 Bollywood movie telling the story of a child with special needs, carried a message for today's parents to be more sensitive to their children and not transfer their own pressures onto the little ones. Viewers left the theater teary-eyed, men and women alike. Blame it on one of the movie's songs, "*Maa*" ("Mom"), a child's narration of his insecurities to his mother when she leaves him alone. To a generation living with the guilt of not bringing up their children the way their parents did, this song dredged up guilt from deep recesses of the heart. The film was a mega hit, and so was the song.

You can use credit/debit to sell anything to the Transition Generation: heart-friendly cooking oil (the message of Safolla from Marico), soaps and shampoos with no side effects, holiday packages as time with family, credit cards and loans as giving back to parents (as pitched by MasterCard Gold in India), or anything else that ties in a little bit of goodness with a little bit of indulgence—pediatric medicines with chocolate flavor, maybe?

The No-Strings Generation: Life Unbound

Comedy has barely been developed as a genre in Bollywood. There have been comedians, all right, and comedy was certainly a part of the multiple courses of emotions that any Indian movie served up. But there were virtually no films whose main purpose was pure entertainment—cinema that's deliberately thin in storyline to make room for enough jokes to be cracked and light-hearted songs to be performed. But then, "having fun" was never one of the values that any previous Indian generation had lived by, either!

In our contacts with the No-Strings Generation, when we probed for the key values that they lived by, "having fun" came up in various ways and words. This generation is certainly clear that life is about fun (among other things, of course), and entertainment need not have deeper meaning to it. No wonder, then, that comedy has become a genre by itself in today's Bollywood. Actors such as Ritesh Deshmukh and Arshad Warsi, directors such as Priyadarshan and David Dhawan, and movies such as *Dhamaal* and *Partner* are the most successful box office performers today, because they deliver two and a half hours of pure fun ("time-pass" as it's called in India).

Mirroring the movies they like, members of the No-Strings Generation want to take life easy. Their take on life is certainly more transactional and self-centered than that of preceding generations. Unlike the Partition Generation, held back by history in many ways, and the Transition Generation, wishing to balance every debit with an equivalent credit, the No-Strings Generation has allegiance only to itself. This clarity of purpose may make many decisions much easier for them. Their value system is more sensitive to their personal needs. As one of them put it during our interactions, "We believe in being honest, but only to ourselves." Staying true to their label, the No-Strings Generation are truly unbound.

So what are the key life principles that the No-Strings Generation lives by, and what do these mean for brands and businesses?

1. Thriving on Discontinuity

Unlike the Partition Generation, which seeks stability in everything from jobs to relationships to brands, the No-Strings Generation thrives on discontinuity and finds stability boring. Although it cannot be denied that this is certainly a function of their current age, all indicators show that as a generation they have a much higher appetite for experimentation. A worldview that looks at life as a series of experiences means that this generation is always on the move: from one relationship to another, from one job to another, from one career to another. It's not surprising that business process outsourcing (BPO), a sector that predominantly employs a younger population, has an average attrition rate of about 30 to 35 percent, according to various industry estimates.[5]

This is a generation that ranks almost everything in life on a linear scale from boring to not boring. As one of them put it in our interactions, "You can't have the same food every day, can you?" He was commenting on the stability of his romantic relationships. Multiple relationships among younger people is certainly not new in the history of India—or of humanity, for that matter—but a decade earlier you would never have expected such a statement to be made so openly in a group. The focus on "I, me, myself" has meant that this generation finds it easy to cut off and move on, which the Partition and Transition generations rarely managed to do.

Brands would therefore do better by factoring in this segment's need for many and varied experiences. Not that they are devoid of brand loyalty. But we would be wise to keep the expiration dates of our ideas shorter and continually strive to move these consumers from one product experience to another. This also means that the market for adventure services and new interests is ripening in India. The Shaimak Davar Institute of Performing Arts (SDIPA), which started in 1992 with just two centers in Mumbai, has grown up to have 13 centers in Mumbai, 7 in Delhi and 4 in Bangalore.[6] This generation's desire for discontinuity is not limited to acquiring lateral skills; it is impacting their choice of others things as well, including career. The challenge is—given a generation looking to explore more in life, for whom the normal is boring—how can we constantly create new experiences and new ways to present old experiences?

2. Elbow Room

Pop star Shakira performed in Mumbai in March 2007. Although there isn't much data available on the profile of people who attended the concert, people who managed to attend described the average age of attendees as 45. Granted, youth and music know no age boundaries, but for the average age to be 45 at a concert by a teenage and youth icon like Shakira is a bit of a shock. Well, perhaps not so shocking when you find out that the tickets to this teen idol show were priced upward of Rs.3,650 ($75), making it not so affordable for those who were perhaps more deserving of being there.

The youth in today's India are feeling a bit of a squeeze. "40 is the new 20" has meant that the 20-somethings have nowhere to go. Because the Transition Generation feels rather young, is learning to let go, and is empowered by rising affluence, their millions end up encroaching on the space that would seem to rightfully belong to the youth. Everybody from 15 to 45 in India today is being seen with the same brands and at the same places. Whether it's a pair of Levis, a casual café, a pop show, or a cool tattoo, nothing is an exclusive marker of the youth. Nothing helps them exclude themselves from their elders.

The No-Strings Generation is seeking to retrieve their space. But their way to do so is more through clever manipulation and negotiation than through direct rebellion. They are finding a way around things rather than against them, managing the system rather than overthrowing it. There's a huge need for brands, products, and services that focus especially on the needs of this generation and help them capture their space by speaking to this approach to life. Candy brands such as Mentos (Perfetti Van Melle) have tried to tap into the innate inventiveness of this generation; the thought, however, is limited to the advertising proposition.

3. Unchecked Optimism

In *Bunty Aur Babli*, a mainstream Bollywood blockbuster of 2005, there is an argument between the modest father, who has worked all his life as a clerk with Indian Railways, and the ambitious son who refuses to go for an interview for the same job. The father, flummoxed by the son's refusal, quizzes him: "So do you think you will become Birla, Tata, or Ambani [the rich industrialists of India]?" The son replies, straight-faced, "Why not? Those guys did not fall from the sky; they also grew up in our kind of environments." "The sky is the limit" is not merely a proverb for this generation; it's a belief. Entrepreneurship and being able to do your own thing a few years down the line is a big theme among the No-Strings Generation. Most of them will eloquently share with you their plans of how they want to work for a few years, get relevant experience, and start their own enterprises.

A sense of optimism without limits certainly means that this is a generation that spends more easily than, say, the Partition Generation. And this optimism is not unfounded, as it is supported at least partially by an impressive earning potential. In February 2008, *Businessworld* reported on the purchasing power of the No-Strings Generation employed with just the

BPO firms in India. According to Nasscom (the trade body and the chamber of commerce of the IT industry in India), the BPO sector employed 245,500 people in 2003–04. Assuming 90 percent of this workforce is below the age of 25 and earns Rs.10,000 a month on average, it puts their purchasing power to no less than Rs.22 billion annually.[7] *YouSumerism*, a report on Indian youth by Ernst & Young Retail Advisory Group, labels the 13- to 21-year-olds "Dabblers." The report presents an equally encouraging spending pattern. According to this study, the Dabblers in cities spend Rs.4,000–5,000 per month on lifestyle products, while their country cousins spend Rs.1,500—3,000 per month.[8]

Is life too good for this segment? This question worries many marketing and advertising people. What can brands and businesses do for a generation that has everything it needs? There are two possible strategies. One is to place an equivalent faith in these consumers' dreams and their confidence in achieving them, by celebrating it through the brands that we use to target them. The other is to devise products and services that help these young people cover the distance between their dreams and making them a reality. The talent shows on Indian television today are doing exactly that. Giving at least a few representative members of this generation a shot at passion, fame, and fortune—all three in one go. Another example is Kota in Rajasthan, which has created a full industry of coaching students for entrance examinations to enter some of the most prestigious engineering and medical institutes in India. Some 50,000 students come only to Kota's IIT coaching institutes from across India every year, giving the industry an annual turnover of around Rs.500 *crores* ($107 million).[9] Kota is leveraging the unchecked optimism of the No-Strings Generation, helping them cover the distance and turn their dreams of becoming a doctor or an engineer into a reality.

4. Bad Is the New Good

Times Life, the *Times of India*'s weekend supplement on lifestyle trends, carried a feature titled "Bad Is the New Good" in December 2007. The article highlighted something that's been happening in the society for some time: the line between what's good and what's bad, what's acceptable and what's not, is blurring for the youth in today's India. In a four-city poll conducted by the national daily in the age group 16 to 25, 74 percent insisted that good or bad is their personal choice, not a matter to be decided by society or anybody else. "If you can't scoop out cream with a straight finger, there is no harm in using a crooked one" is how someone from the No-Strings Generation encapsulated their philosophy in life in one of our interactions.

The No-Strings generation certainly has a more transactional and practical view of the world than the other two generations. "We don't want to be serious about our relationships, as this is our time to focus on our careers," said one in our interactions. Added another: "Honesty and hard work by themselves are not good enough in today's world; you need to be smart and diplomatic to get your work done." In these times of blurring boundaries, one of the biggest challenges for brands is to realize that the No-Strings Generation will not readily identify with a spokesperson whitewashed with goodness. A little dash of mischief, a hint of manipulation in the characters and the brands makes them so much more real for this segment. This is the time of antiheroes in India. Take a look at the mischievous smile of Akshay Kumar, the favorite Bollywood actor of this generation, and you will know what "bad is the new good" means to them.

Unlocking New Opportunities

There is potential at the two ends of the age spectrum in India—certainly much more than what we are cumulatively tapping right now. As it appears from this analysis, this potential is not only significant but also distinct from the mainstream on which we have been focusing. India is not just young; it's also older and younger. The big Indian opportunity is not one monolith but three distinct segments with their own worldviews and consumption needs. There are real reasons for these three segments to believe and behave differently, as their driving influences are so very different, summarized in Figure 10.3.

Figure 10.3. Three Segments and Their Key Life Themes.

Segment	Partition Generation 45 to 64	Transition Generation 25 to 44	No Strings Generation 15 to 24
Life Themes	Held back, but not holding back	Letting go	Thriving on discontinuity
	Desire for permanence	Chasing tomorrow	Elbow room
	A high regard for functionality	Reconciling the dilemma of change	Unchecked optimism
	Community as a key support	Credit/debit living	Bad is the new good

There is always safety in numbers, in doing what everybody else is doing. This leads to a mainstream myopia among marketers. But time and again, markets have woken up to realize that there's potential beyond the mainstream that is not essentially niche. Take, for example, the idea of "the fortune at the bottom of the pyramid" first unveiled by C. K. Prahalad, which is now beginning to bear fruit. The bottom-of-the-pyramid opportunity found its first tangible shape in Nano, a car for the masses designed by Tata Motors in India to retail at Rs.100,000 ($2,000). This triggered a surge in marketers who have come alive to this opportunity and have announced their plans to tap this segment. The potential fortune at the bottom of the market is on its way to becoming a reality.

The cultural mélange that is India today—three distinct generations, three different worldviews—will not change dramatically in the frame of 10 years or so, but it will inevitably continue to evolve, shaped by further, as yet unknown events. If we as marketers don't take in the full breadth of desires and demands that India offers today, we will miss out on opportunities that are alive and ready—and may well be a limited-time offer.

Based on this understanding, we can not only take advantage of new opportunities but also find new ways of handling old opportunities. For instance, is there a scope for brands in India that target only the No-Strings Generation, perhaps to the exclusion of everyone else? What could be the business model for such a brand? How can we deliver discontinuity to this segment in product, pricing, and service? What about the education market in India? What about fashion brands only for the youth? What about a chain of dating restaurants? Would a business house want to enter these highly profitable segments in an organized way, just as they decide to enter the insurance category—or the FMCG for that matter?

Similarly, do all banks need to look young and technological? In the market where cold efficiency is replacing warm service and unsmiling tellers are directing you to the ATM, should the biggest bank in the country run an advertising campaign about its surprising facts and figures—or the comforting warmth of its tea? Do the Partition Generation and a large part of the Transition Generation prefer technological coldness or personal warmth? Also, when everybody from Olay to Garnier to Pond's is selling anti-aging products to 30-year-olds, is there a market for helping the older beauties look younger? More than that, is there room for a line of personal grooming products specially designed for the needs of an aging skin?

The list of questions and subsequent opportunities is long and self-generating. The bigger question, however, is this: do we want to spread our wings more widely? Are we willing to let go of our baggage and open ourselves to the new? Do we look at this opportunity and behave like the No-Strings Generation, saying "Let's leap!" or do we behave like the Partition Generation, saying "Let me think about it"? The choice is ours to make.

NOTES

Chapter 1

1. Somini Sengupta, "India's 'Idol' Recipe: Mix Small-Town Grit and Democracy," *Mumbai Journal*, May 25, 2006, www.nytimes.com
2. Freedonia Group, "World Architectural Paints to 2011," February 2008, 108–110.
3. ASSOCHAM, "Prospects for Ayurvedic and Medical Tourism Industries During CWG 2010," March 19, 2008.
4. V. Pandit Ranjit, "What's Next for Tata Group? An Interview with Its Chairman," *McKinsey Quarterly*, 2005, 4, 62.

Chapter 2

1. Swati Sharma, "Big Jump in Indians Travelling Overseas," November 21, 2009, http://indiatoday.intoday.in/site/Story/71766/Business/Big+jump+in+Indians+travelling+overseas.html
2. BS Reporter, "High Rates Hit Home Loans Growth," January 29, 2008, http://www.business-standard.com/india/news/high-rates-hit-home-loans-growth/311901/
3. PTI, "Average Age of House Owners Drops to 30 from 55: ASSOCHAM," November 4, 2007, http://www.livemint.com/2007/11/04133925/Average-age-of-house-owners-dr.html
4. Insurance Regulatory and Development Authority (IRDA), total life insurance premiums from 2001–2002 to 2007–2008 (in Rs. *crores*), new policies issued 2002–2003 to 2007–2008.

Chapter 3

1. Dheeraj Sinha, "Changing Face of Beauty in India," Bates Enterprise India, December 2006.
2. Ibid.

3. Usha Sharma, "Evergreen Horizon," November 15, 2009, http://www.expresspharmaonline.com/20091115/market01.shtml

4. Media Research Users Council (MRUC), Indian Readership Survey 2008, Fairness Cream Usage 2007–2008, Age-wise.

5. Sinha, "Changing Face of Beauty in India."

6. FICCI–Ernst & Young, "Wellness: Exploring the Untapped Potential," April 2009.

7. Indrajit Basu, "Indian Men Looking Good," January 12, 2006, http://www.atimes.com/atimes/South_Asia/HA12Df03.html

8. IANS, "Indian Men Take to Fairness Creams," May 25, 2010, http://timesofindia.indiatimes.com/life-style/beauty/Indian-men-take-to-fairness-creams/articleshow/5972296.cms

9. Press Trust of India, "Elder Group Co Eyes 8% Share in Men's Grooming," March 25, 2009, http://www.business-standard.com/india/news/elder-group-co-eyes-8-share-in-men%5Cs-grooming/57319/on

Chapter 4

1. Ambez Media & Market Research, "How Cable TV Began and Spread in India," 1999, http://indiancabletv.net/cabletvhistory.htm; FICCI-KPMG, "Back in the Spotlight: Indian Media & Entertainment Industry Report," 2010, pp. 41, 44.

2. PricewaterhouseCoopers, "Indian Entertainment and Media Outlook" report, 2009.

3. "Indian Readership Survey Q1 2010: Dainik Jagran, TOI Lead Among Dailies; Saras Salil, India Today Top Magazines," May 4, 2010, http://www.exchange4media.net/e4m/news/fullstory.asp?section_id=5&news_id=38031&tag=3633

4. "This Year, Next Year: India Media Forecasts," Group M, Spring 2009, p. 10.

5. Krishna Gopalan, "The Force of the Fourth," *Economic Times*, August 15, 2009, p. 16.

Chapter 5

1. Sriram Srinivasan, "Clicking Together—Matrimonial Sites Are Unique to India and the Two Main Players Are Profitable," May 31, 2008, Outlook Business, p. 63.

2. "'Common Man' to Endorse Air Deccan," May 5, 2005, http://www.thehindubusinessline.com/2005/05/05/stories/2005050501590400.htm

3. Tribune News Service, "Air Deccan Ties Up with Reliance WebWorld," August 3, 2005, http://www.tribuneindia.com/2005/20050803/biz.htm#3

4. Hemali Chhapia, "Communication Gap Led to E-Mess," August 5, 2009, http://timesofindia.indiatimes.com/city/mumbai/Communication-gap-led-to-e-mess/articleshow/4857978.cms

5. "LG Launches New Refrigerator Line-Up," March 20, 2010, http://www.thehindubusinessline.com/2010/03/20/stories/2010032053360500.htm

6. Ibid.

7. Barun Jha, "Samsung Targets Multi-fold Surge in LED TV Sales in India," August 7, 2009, http://www.livemint.com/2009/08/07155956/Samsung-targets-multifold-sur.html

8. "Maruti Suzuki Launches Estilo with K-series Engine and Bold New Design," August 25, 2009, http://www.marutisuzuki.com/Maruti-Suzuki-launches-Estilo-with-K-series-engine-and-bold-new-design.aspx

Chapter 6

1. NCAER, "The Next Urban Frontier: Twenty Cities To Watch," 2008, http://www.ncaer.org/downloads/journals/macrotrack_august2008.pdf

2. FICCI–Ernst & Young, "Wellness: Exploring the Untapped Potential," April 2009.

3. C. K. Prahalad, "Fortune at the Bottom of the Pyramid, The: Eradicating Poverty Through Profits" Jan 27, 2006, Wharton School Publishing, pp. 3–7.

4. "Jyothy Laboratories—Who We Are," 2007, http://www.jyothylaboratories.com/whoweare.aspx

5. Press Trust of India, "Max Bupa Health Insurance to Infuse Rs 550 cr in Five Yrs," May 2, 2010, http://www.business-standard.com/india/news/max-bupa-health-insurance-to-infuse-rs-550-cr-in-five-yrs/93038/on

6. Bart Minten & Ashok Gulati, "From Mandi to Market," September 2, 2009, http://timesofindia.indiatimes.com/home/opinion/edit-page/Top-Article-From-Mandi-To-Market/articleshow/4960251.cms

Chapter 8

1. Somini Sengupta, "In India, Women See Boxing as a Way Up," August 25, 2009, http://www.nytimes.com/2009/08/26/sports/global/26boxing.html

2. Reeba Zachariah, "Moms Get a Chance to Be Managers Again," August 10, 2009, http://timesofindia.indiatimes.com/news/business/india-business/Moms-get-a-chance-to-be-managers-again/article show/4875427.cms

3. RNCOS, "Women Wear Market Forecast to 2010," August 2008, http://www.rncos.com/Report/IM127.htm

Chapter 9

1. PTI, "Indian Economy Up 6.7% in FY09," May 29, 2009, http://www.businessworld.in/index.php/Economy/Indian-Economy-Up.html

2. India Knowledge@Wharton, "Why Companies See Bright Prospects in Rural India," June 18, 2009, http://knowledge.wharton.upenn.edu/india/article.cfm?articleid=4386

3. Techtree News Staff, "India's Rural Mobile Subscribers Rise," July 14, 2009, http://www.rimweb.in/forums/topic/19017-telecom-sub scriber-base-count-in-india/

4. India Knowledge@Wharton, "Why Companies See Bright Prospects."

5. Ibid.

6. Ankit Ajmera, "101 Markets 2008: The Immense Potential of Small Town India," March 20, 2008, http://www.afaqs.com/perl/news/story.html?sid=20666

7. India Knowledge@Wharton, "An Increasingly Affluent Middle India Is Harder to Ignore," July 10, 2008, http://knowledge.wharton.upenn.edu/india/article.cfm?articleid=4303

8. India Knowledge@Wharton, "What Makes Titan Tick? Finding Opportunity in India's Unorganized Retail Sector," January 22, 2009, http://knowledge.wharton.upenn.edu/india/article.cfm?articleid=4348

9. CNN-IBN "Are Small Towns India's Ticket to the Big League?" August 8, 2007, http://ibnlive.in.com/news/are-small-towns-indias-ticket-to-the-big-league/46419-19.html

10. Kalpesh Damor, "McCain Foods May Start Potato Farming in Kutch," March 7, 2008, http://www.business-standard.com/india/news/mccain-foods-may-start-potato-farming-in-kutch/316046/

11. Latha Jishnu, "The New Middle Man," http://www.businessworld
.in/index.php/Retail-FMCG/The-New-Middle-Man.html

Chapter 10

1. Bella Jaisinghani, "Life Begins at 60," *Times of India*, February
2008.
2. PTI, "LIC Housing Finance to Launch Care Homes for Aged,"
December 28, 2008, http://www.livemint.com/2008/12/28104341/
LIC-Housing-Finance-to-launch.html
3. "Turnaround: Big B Revitalises Chyawanprash Category,"
January 26, 2004, http://www.financialexpress.com/news/
turnaround-big-b-revitalises-chyawanprash-category/89270/
4. Naazneen Karmali, "Fabindia," February 16, 2009, http://www
.forbes.com/global/2009/0216/024a.html
5. *Deccan Herald*, "BPO Summit in India to Focus on Attrition,
Merger Issues," July 6, 2006, http://www.nasscom.in/Nasscom/
templates/NormalPage.aspx?id=1548
6. http://www.sdipa.com/
7. Rashmi Bansal, "A New Face of Youth Consumerism,"
February 2008, http://www.businessworld.in/index.php/
A-new-face-of-youth-consumerism.html
8. Ernst & Young Retail Advisory Group, "YouSumerism, Youth in
India—Opportunity Knocks!" 2007, p. 6.
9. Rakhee Roy Talukdar, "Top 10 Ranks Elude Kota," May 27,
2010, http://www.telegraphindia.com/1100527/jsp/nation/story_
12492737.jsp

INDEX